BERRY BOYS

BERRY BOYS

Portraits of First World War Soldiers and Families

Michael Fitzgerald and Claire Regnault

First published in New Zealand in 2014 by Te Papa Press
PO Box 467, Wellington, New Zealand
www.tepapapress.co.nz

Text © Museum of New Zealand Te Papa Tongarewa
Images © Museum of New Zealand Te Papa Tongarewa, or as credited below

This book is copyright. Apart from any fair dealing for the purpose of private study, research, criticism, or review, as permitted under the Copyright Act, no part of this book may be reproduced by any process, stored in a retrieval system, or transmitted in any form, without the prior permission of the Museum of New Zealand Te Papa Tongarewa.

TE PAPA® is the trademark of the Museum of New Zealand Te Papa Tongarewa
Te Papa Press is an imprint of the Museum of New Zealand Te Papa Tongarewa

All images in the plates section, those on the front and back cover and on pages v, vii, 2, 4–5, 7, 12–13 and 16–17 by Berry & Co.
Photography on pages viii–1 and 8 by Michael Hall, and on page 15 by Norman Heke, Te Papa.
Image on page 2 from the collection of Jill Helson.
Object on page 11 from Finnis House Collection, photographed by Museum Theatre Gallery, Napier.
Images on pages 3, 9 (lower) and 14 from the Alexander Turnbull Library, Wellington.
Image on page 9 (top) from Sir George Grey Special Collections, Auckland Libraries.

A catalogue record for this book is available from the National Library of New Zealand
ISBN 978-0-9941041-2-0

Design by Spencer Levine
Digital imaging by Jeremy Glyde
Printed by Mainprint, Auckland, a division of Ultimo Group

Published with the generous support of Wellington City Council's WW100 commemorative programme and Ultimo Group.

Contents

Introduction 1

Plates 17

Acknowledgements 184

Notes 186

Bibliography 187

Index 189

To look at photographs of people is to engage in a kind of mourning for past innocence, their poignancy sharpened in the knowledge of what was to come. In war photography these responses are magnified. Danger hovers at the edges of all such images ... The possibility of dying that is their subtext, for their subjects as much as the photographer, means they make urgent claims on our attention ...

Caroline Brothers, *War and Photography* [1]

Forgotten ephemera still being found in 147 Cuba Street testifies to the building's fifty-year history as a photographic studio.

Introduction

Lost and found

In the 1980s Delia Grace, an art dealer, moved into the upper floor of one of Wellington's old Cuba Street buildings. While renovating the ceiling space, Delia came across a cache of thousands of glass plate negatives and a scattering of old business ephemera. It was an astounding discovery and evidence of the building's long history as a home of photography.

Thanks in part to the beautiful quality of the natural light that pours through its windows, 147 Cuba Street has been synonymous with dealer art galleries since 1968, when Peter McLeavey established his groundbreaking gallery. It began its creative life, however, as the photographic studio of William Berry (1857–1949), who founded the building in 1900. The building housed a succession of photographers throughout the first half of the twentieth century. While traces of the capital's once-bustling photographic industry have virtually disappeared from Wellington's streets, 'Berry & Co. Photographers' remains proudly emblazoned across the building's façade.

The façade of 147 Cuba Street still bears the Berry & Co. legend.

The found negatives include photographs not only by the Berry studio, but also by the company's successors, including Henri Harrison, R Goetzlof and Cuba Photographers. Combined, they open up a fascinating window on the past: traversing the changing face of everyday New Zealanders from 1900 to the late 1940s, they reaffirm the desire of individuals and families to document important moments in their lives. Significantly, the negatives also span two world wars and include portraits of men dressed in military uniform from both conflicts.

The surviving negatives by Berry & Co. include 194 portraits of First World War soldiers – no doubt just a small proportion of the total number Berry actually took. The portraits show seventy-two individual soldiers, ranging in age from seventeen to sixty-five, as well as seventeen couples, including five wedding portraits, and fourteen family groups. While the majority hail from the greater Wellington area, others come from as far away as Helensville in the north and Dunedin in the south, reflecting the numbers of men who came to Wellington to train and embark. They range from the respectable (a clergyman) to the inglorious (a prisoner); from the everyday (working-class men, farmers, labourers and storemen) to the unexpected (a jockey and theatrical agent). While the sample is small, and by no means unique,[2] the stories of the individual soldiers and the roles they played in the war, from gunners to bakers, are remarkable in their diversity. The collection puts a human face on war and reinforces the commemorative role that photography serves, especially in times of crisis.

The stairwell of 147 Cuba Street as it is today.

Berry & Co.

By the turn of the twentieth century, studio portraiture was well established in New Zealand, with competition between studios frequently resulting in price wars.[3] While studio photography had once been the preserve of the well-to-do, technological advances during the late nineteenth century had democratised the genre and made it affordable to the masses. A bargain hunter could sit for a single cabinet photograph for two shillings and six pence.[4] William Berry established his first studio in 1899 at 64 Cuba Street, following his acquisition of the New Zealand Photographic Company, for whom he had worked since 1896. William Berry came to the business from the newspaper world; he had been a compositor at the *Evening Post* since his early twenties.[5] At forty-two years of age, however, Berry had ambitious plans for his new career, starting with a purpose-built studio.

By 1900 Berry had raised enough money to engage the popular Wellington architect William Crichton to design a three-storey building at 147 Cuba Street that would house a new photographic studio and shop. In March 1901, Berry announced the opening of his 'most modern' and to 'up-to-date' premises in the *Free Lance*.[6] The new building at 147 Cuba Street featured a ground floor shop, which Berry rented out, and a display case for the company's work.[7] Customers were invited to leave the hustle and bustle of the street behind, and to make their way up the stairs to the first-floor reception, where they were greeted by Mrs Berry, or one of the couple's daughters.[8]

This cabinet card depicts William and Elizabeth 'Lizzie' Berry, with their four daughters (left to right) Mabel, Ethel, Beatrice and Florence. Emblazoned with the legends of both the New Zealand Photographic Company and Berry & Co., it was produced at the turn of the century as Berry transitioned the company.

Sarah Coombridge (up ladder) and Christina McAllister working in James McAllister's photographic studio in Stratford in 1905 - a glimpse into the interior of a typical New Zealand photographic studio, with its pitched glass roof and choice of backdrops and props.

Depending on the number of sitters and the nature of their portraits, clients would then be escorted to either the large studio on the first floor or the smaller studio on the second floor, which featured a sloping glass roof for natural light. Generous dressing rooms, in which to primp, preen and make final adjustments to outfits, were adjacent to both. The magic of creating a print also took place on the premises. Berry used pre-prepared gelatin dry plate negatives, a process that was in common usage by the late 1880s and which enabled photographers to produce highly detailed prints. While the negatives were developed on the first floor, toning, enlarging and retouching took place in rooms on the second. Retouching was a common, if at times controversial, practice. Since studios sought to produce the most flattering likenesses possible for their clients, retouchers removed small 'defects', such as skin blemishes, with the aid of a graphite pencil.

Whereas the New Zealand Photographic Company had offered 'Photography for the People'[9] and 'the cheapest and the best',[10] Berry sought to position his company as a first-class creator of 'artistic' portraits, and as a specialist in bridal groups.[11] As such, he made direct appeals to the ladies of Wellington in many of his early advertisements, including an announcement in 1902 that the studio had acquired the services of a ladies' hairdresser who would be 'at the command of patrons' for no extra fee.[12] But while Berry certainly attracted a coterie of fashionably attired women, he too was a photographer of the people. Rather than the upper echelons, 'his customers were ordinary Wellingtonians, tradespeople and their families'.[13]

Berry & Co. offered sitters a range of stylistic options for their portraits, from a straightforward head and shoulders shot against a plain background, to a romantic portrait with diffused lighting, or something more aristocratic. The studio was equipped, as were most, with a selection of scenic canvas backdrops, including grand European interiors decorated with marble columns, candelabra and great swathes of luxuriant fabric; ivy-draped terraces; and tree-framed views of picturesque landscapes. The studio also provided sitters with a familiar selection of props, including tables and chairs (useful for arranging and supporting children), a faux set of stairs with an ornate balustrade, rugs, flowers, books, papers, and even writing instruments. Within this make-believe environment, indoor props and outdoor backdrops happily coexisted. The glass plates reveal the demarcation between fantasy and reality as the edges of the painted canvas, wrinkled floor coverings and studio equipment come into view. In the printing room, such extraneous information was carefully cropped out, so that the resulting photograph focused squarely on the sitter.

In 1902, Berry & Co. began offering 'artistic' portraits and the services of a ladies' hairdresser. These portraits of a woman with an elaborate coiffure were commissioned under the name 'Hogg'. Cropped, the close-up would have been perfect for an oval locket.

This group of portraits, dating from 1900 to 1920, shows the range of props and highly aspirational backdrops open to customers of Berry & Co. Many people posed in costume.

G. R.

"We are fighting for a worthy purpose, and we shall not lay down our arms until that purpose has been fully achieved."

THE KING

MEN OF THE EMPIRE
TO ARMS!

GOD SAVE THE KING!

Men in uniform

Amongst the portraits of women dressed in their finery, children in their Sunday best and families, two other types of portrait emerge: men, women and children delighting in the spirit of fancy dress, and those in uniform. The latter include constables, nurses, clergymen, Salvation Army officers, cadets and even a postie. The most numerous men in uniform, however, are rank-and-file soldiers: ordinary men – farmers, grocers, storemen, clerks – newly dressed for their roles in the British Empire's Great War. On 8 August 1914, just four days after Britain declared war on Germany, the New Zealand Government called for volunteers for an expeditionary force.[14] Ten days later, the *Dominion* reported that 4500 men from the Wellington military district had already signed up.[15] On 16 October, amidst great fanfare and the strains of 'It's a Long Way to Tipperary', 8534 newly trained soldiers set sail from Wellington Harbour for a war that many believed would be over by Christmas. In the lead-up to their departure, thousands of soldiers from all around New Zealand had their portrait taken in their brand-new uniforms.

Commissioned under the name 'Harris' this photograph features a young corporal in the Girl Peace Scouts. Founded in 1908, and under the patronage of Lady Liverpool (wife of the governor and enthusiastic wartime fundraiser), the Girl Peace Scouts used their skills to support the war effort, including knitting for the troops, rolling bandages for hospital ships and holding concerts to raise funds for sick and wounded soldiers.

The photographic event of the century

The Great War, it has been argued, was the 'photographic event of the century' due to the role that photography played in the lives of combatants, not least in the way everyday soldiers documented their own wartime experiences with a camera.[16] An American songwriting trio captured the relationship between the soldier and his camera in the popular song 'When I Send You a Picture of Berlin', in which they described Johnny Johnson, 'feeling fit [in his] uniform and army kit', as a 'cam'ra fiend'.

> When I send you a picture of London
> Then you'll know I've landed safely 'Over There'
> When I've sent you a snapshot of Paris
> You'll know I'm ready to do and dare (I'll do my share)
>
> You'll know I'm thinking about you
> When I send you my photo all alone
> But when I send you a picture of Berlin
> You'll know it's over, 'Over There' I'm coming home.[17]

As the song implies, soldiers used photography, as well as the written word, as a means of sharing their war experiences with loved ones, and maintaining a connection between home and away. The relationship

The Parliamentary Recruiting Committee in Britain produced this poster in 1914 to encourage voluntary enlistment. It went on display in Britain and across the empire.

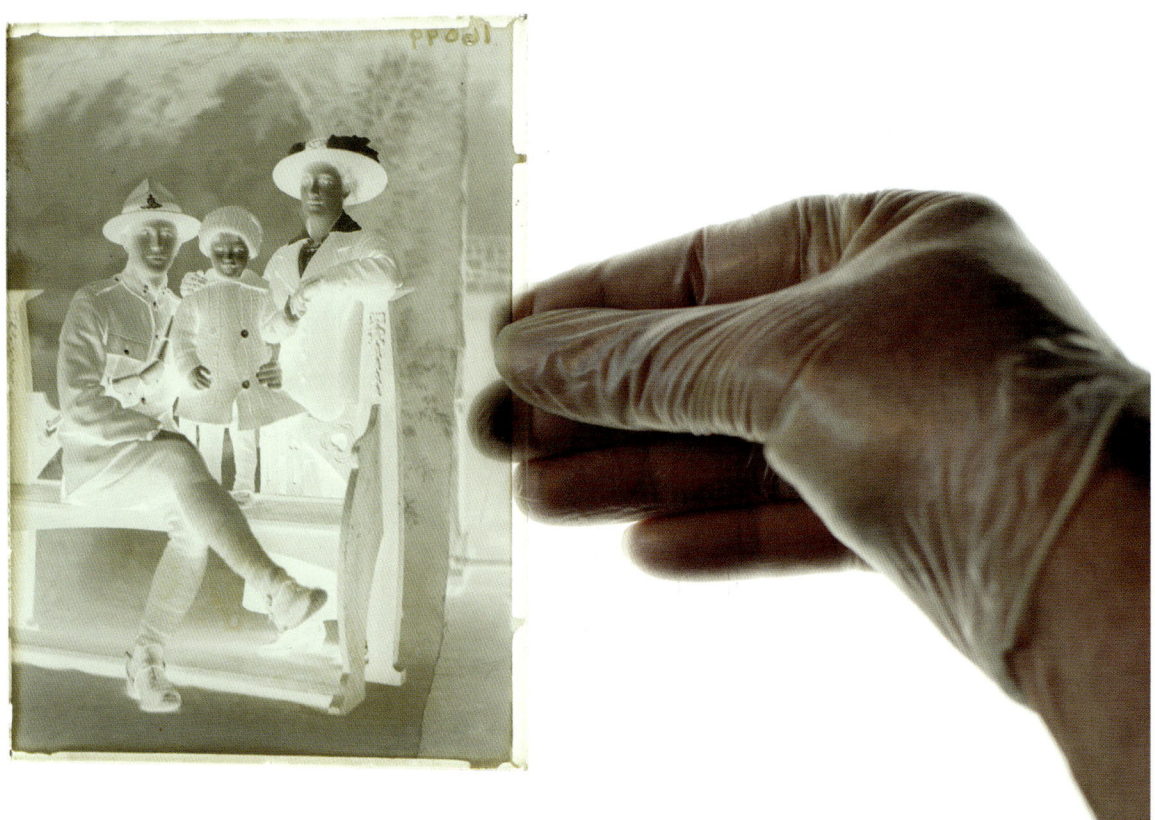

Berry & Co. used prepared gelatin glass plate negatives. Glass plate negatives were in popular use from the late 1880s through to the 1920s, although some photographers continued to use them into the 1970s. This is one of two negatives featuring Walter and Ida Scambary and their young son George.

between a serviceman and his camera was encouraged by companies such as Kodak, who marketed the Soldier's Kodak in 1916, and by professional photographers, a number of whom even set up business in training camps around the country.

From a commercial perspective, William Berry was well aware of the opportunities a war presented a professional photographer based in the capital. In January 1900, as soldiers left for South Africa to fight for the empire and 'the flag',[18] Berry took his cameras to the street to document the contingent's grand send-off from Wellington. He shot the 'only views taken showing His Excellency the Governor and Premier addressing the Contingent', and sold them for two shillings each, in a move described by the *Evening Post* reporter as 'a smart bit of work'.[19] This is something that Berry perhaps learned from his predecessors at the New Zealand Photographic Company, who in 1888, as changes were being made to the organisation of the country's military forces, had called for 'Volunteers in Uniform' to be photographed in groups or separately.[20]

Despite the increasing popularity of home photography in the early 1900s, following the introduction of photographic film and affordable box cameras such as the Brownie, New Zealanders continued to value the superior quality of formal studio portraits as markers of significant occasions. The transition of an ordinary civilian into a soldier was such an occasion. The majority of the portraits in the Berry collection are of individual soldiers, many of whom probably walked into the studio off the street. They often posed for at least two frames – most commonly one seated, one standing. Other soldiers visited the studio with family members, no doubt arriving by specific appointment. An appointment would allow time not only for outfits and accessories to be carefully chosen, but also for multiple compositions to be arranged and shot, including individual portraits and various family groupings, both of which often included hats on and hats off.

Shorthand inscriptions on the glass plates, such as 'Cab 6' or 'PC 12', show that the soldiers ordered a range of formats and multiple prints. Twelve copies was a popular order. Cabinet prints, mounted on a trade card and measuring 4 by 5-and-a-half inches (10 by 12 centimetres), were on a scale that was both displayable and portable, while postcards were easy to send by mail. Those who could afford it ordered twelve-by-ten-inch (30-by-25-centimetre) prints destined for framing. The ritual of sitting for a photograph and then distributing the prints features in many letters and diaries of the period. Arthur Sims, due to depart from his home town of Auckland on 17 November 1917, recorded the hectic final days of leave in his diary. Amid a busy schedule of lunches, afternoon teas, dinners and trips to the movies, he fitted in a visit to Crown Studios for a photo. Four days later, he picked up his prints and began distributing them, noting who he gave them to.[21] Meanwhile, Bert Stokes, a junior clerk from Wellington who left for the war in 1916, informed his mother in no uncertain terms that she could order as many photographs as she liked, but he wanted 'about half a dozen to give away outside of relations'.[22] His letter included a list of female recipients. Photographs of loved ones proved equally important to Bert while at the front. He gratefully wrote to his mother, 'I am so glad you had that photo of you done for me. There's never a day goes by without I have to look at it.'[23] In a moving letter to his wife, Ida, from Gallipoli in June 1915, Colonel William Malone wrote, 'I am sitting at a biscuit box escritoire with your dear photo at my right hand.'

In homes across New Zealand, soldier portraits were transformed into keepsakes to be displayed, held and caressed – some close to the body, secured in lockets kept warm by the skin. Cabinet cards and framed portraits sat on the mantelpiece at the heart of the home – a focal point for pride, prayers and remembrance. The importance of portraits as emotional touchstones is reflected in the popular iconography of the time, with newspapers featuring scenes that typically show a woman – a mother, sister or fiancée – communing with a soldier portrait, from gently clasping a picture as she writes, to bowing in front of one in despair after reading a casualty list. As bodies were not returned to be grieved over and buried, soldier portraits came to play an integral role in the mourning process, with many household mantelpieces becoming 'photographic mausoleums'.[24]

Framed portraits of soldiers frequently appear in images of the home during wartime. This *Auckland Weekly News* cover from 16 December 1915 was entitled 'A Christmas Greeting from New Zealand to an Absent One'.

For soldiers fighting in a foreign land, photographs of loved ones provided a tangible sense of home, as can be seen from this snapshot of George Denniston's dugout on Gallipoli.

As Colonel Malone and Bert Stokes' letters home clearly demonstrate, photographic portraits were just as important to the men on active service as to those at home. Snapshots taken by soldiers of their dugouts at the front show photographs of families and sweethearts pinned above their rudimentary beds – the first thing they saw when they woke and the last thing before they slept. As historian Raphael Samuel has asserted, photographs become all the more important among the 'geographically mobile and sociologically orphaned, as a way of reaffirming family roots'.[26] Soldiers also carried small-scale photographs of loved ones into battle, although some expressed concern that these might fall into the hands of the enemy should anything happen to them.[26] Men retrieved photographs, along with other personal possessions, from the bodies of their dead mates, and photographs feature prominently in official lists of dead soldiers' personal effects.

A tax on sons

While it is easy to imagine soldiers enthusiastically bounding up the stairs of the Berry studio in 1914, it soon became a different story. In the early stages of the war, neither those who enlisted nor their families had any concept of the brutality of modern industrialised warfare. Rather, many viewed the war 'as a great adventure that offered them the chance of travel, glamour and glory'.[27] The ill-fated Gallipoli campaign, which lasted from 25 April 1915 to late December of the same year, swiftly changed that outlook. The New Zealand forces suffered over 8000 casualties, including 2700 deaths.[28] The first casualties were reported in the country's newspapers in May: 194 dead, 1405 wounded.[30] In some papers casualty lists were accompanied by a grid of cropped studio portraits, sourced from grieving families, and so the private became public in a display of collective mourning for the nation's loss, not simply a family's.

On 15 July 1915, the people of Wellington saw for their own eyes the real cost of war when they went down to the harbour to meet the *Willochra*. Whereas the ship had left the harbour full of young men in their prime, it returned with a cargo of more than 200 sick and wounded.[31] The sight of the soldiers, including amputees, being assisted off the ship must have been a shock not only for their families, but also for new enlisters. However, as the numbers of wounded and dead mounted, social pressure for men to serve increased. Historian James Belich argues that 'there appears to have been a conception of family sacrifice, a tax on sons that should be evenly shared'.[32] Some men, however, managed to slip through the system. As the war dragged on and the demand for men increased, the military also lowered their

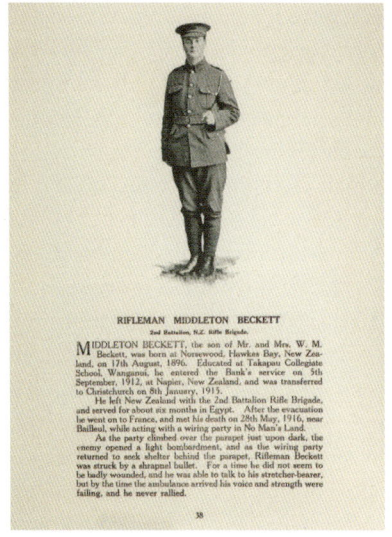

While created for personal use, soldier portraits found their way into the public arena through the lists of war dead. Middleton Beckett's portrait, taken by Berry & Co. in 1915, was clear-cut and printed in the Bank of New South Wales' Roll of Honour following his death in France in 1916.

This fretwork frame, chosen or perhaps made by the people who loved William Gempton (1890–1979), expresses their feelings for William and his contribution to King and country. The photographer of the portrait is not known, but many framed portraits by Berry & Co. would likewise have held a place of pride in the homes of families.

standards, accepting men who had failed their first medical examination. The Berry collection contains portraits of numerous men who served despite medical problems, unsettling the myth of the strapping Anzac.

The majority of Berry's surviving soldier portraits date from the period following the introduction of conscription on 1 August 1916. The first ballots of eligible single men took place in Routh's Building in Brandon Street, Wellington, on 16 November 1916. Under the headline 'Conscription! The Gamble of Human Life', the *NZ Truth* described the proceedings of the first ballot, bitterly observing that after single men and 'men of the first division' had been drawn by ballot, and 'are used up, or have done their bit, even if it be their lives, men of the second division will be torn from their wives and their children to go and win the war over the starting of which . . . politicians in Britain and Germany are still arguing'.[33]

The following year, married men saw their names go into the ballot. Unsurprisingly, group shots are more prevalent in the Berry collection from 1916 onwards. Mothers and sisters protectively flank soldier sons and brothers. Newly-weds pose stiffly. Children physically connect husbands and wives. One of the most affecting family portraits is of the Simpsons (see page 130), who hold their child, with teddy, snugly between them. Leaning her head on her child, she looks content and dreamy, while he smiles. A stark comparison to the stiff formality of other family portraits, Berry's picture of the Simpsons and their easy intimacy is more akin to a snapshot. It perhaps marks a reunion rather than a separation.

While soldier fathers are present, fathers of soldiers are conspicuously absent from the Berry collection. Perhaps fathers found it difficult to take time off work to get to the studio, although there are plenty of other employed men in the collection; or perhaps it reveals that the photographic ritual was more important to the women in the family.

William Berry and his staff would have known the families of many of his sitters, such as the Hornig brothers, who ran a gentlemen's outfitters at 160 Cuba Street, for Wellington had a population of just over 70,000. Berry was also an active man in the community, involved not only in photography but also in yachting, chess, bowls, the Masonic Lodge and even the Wellington Poultry, Pigeon and Canary Society. As a father of four girls – Mabel, Beatrice, Ethel and Florence – Berry did not have to pay any 'tax on sons'. His household, however, would have felt the effects of the war and the anxiety caused by separation. Florence, who was twenty-three in 1914, had fallen in love with a visiting Australian gymnast, Claude Heward, who had arrived in Wellington in early 1911 to take up the position of physical director at the YMCA.[35]

William Berry's future son-in-law Claude Heward (in the dark shorts) and his YMCA gymnastics group perform for the camera during a visit to Berry & Co. for a photoshoot. Originally from Adelaide, Claude signed up to the Australian Imperial Force in August 1914 and served as a gunner.

Kathleen O'Brien is dressed as a soldier for a patriotic revue in 1914-15. During the early stages of the war, theatre groups often created tableaux featuring performers dressed as soldiers and nurses. As the war dragged on, however, such fund-raising events came under fire as unease mounted around having fun while others were fighting for King and country.

Following the outbreak of war, Claude shelved his plans to go to America, and attested for service in his home town of Adelaide on 19 August 1914.³⁶ Following the later call for all able-bodied married men, Mabel and Beatrice's husbands, both of whom were fathers, also enlisted.

On 13 October 1916, William Berry, of 'photographic fame', is recorded as having given a rousing patriotic speech at the opening of the 1916–17 bowling season at the Wellington Bowling Club. Though it was a celebratory occasion, the war was at the forefront of his mind. In October 1916, New Zealanders witnessed the country's highest monthly death toll to date, with 1237 killed and 2969 wounded, many in the Battle of the Somme.³⁷ Berry made a strong appeal to members to raise money for the Soldiers' Christmas Gift Fund, and ended his speech by calling for 'three cheers for the "boys at the front"'.³⁸ He no doubt knew by then that Florence's beloved Claude was hospitalised in England, having suffered a gunshot wound to the thigh and gas poisoning in France two months prior.³⁹

What must these men, and the women who often accompanied them to their sitting, have been thinking when they climbed the stairs to the Berry studio? As they combed their hair, adjusted their uniform and arranged themselves for the camera, the new soldiers must have been all too aware that they were potentially posing for their memorial shot. And what did Berry say to the men and their families, among them new brides, tots and babies, who came to call in greater numbers as the war raged on? Perhaps rather than offer words of comfort, William and his wife Lizzie put their faith in the photographic ritual, realising that their greatest gift to the families was to create the best likeness they could as an aide-mémoire and 'evidence of service and sacrifice';⁴⁰ understanding that the very business of taking a photograph, war or not, 'is to participate in another person's . . . mortality, vulnerability, mutability'.⁴¹

The Peace

Thankfully for families throughout New Zealand, the Armistice was announced on 11 November 1918. Mabel and Beatrice's husbands were never called up. Florence Berry's fiancé Claude survived almost four long years of fighting and hospitalisation, and returned to Australia in February 1918, albeit the worse for wear. A year after his first injury, Claude received a gunshot wound to the face while fighting in Belgium in August 1917. As a result, he lost an eye. Conscious of his disfigurement, he wrote to Florence to say that he did not expect her to follow through with the engagement. Florence, however, was resolute, and the couple married in Adelaide on 22 June 1918.⁴² With 'The Peace'

A group in fancy dress, including 'John Bull', during the Armistice Day celebrations in Levin, 13 November 1918.

Armistice Day parade, Masterton, 1918.

declared, the stream of soldiers to 147 Cuba Street came to an end – at least for the next twenty years, until men enlisted for the Second World War visited the studios. William Berry, who was sixty-one at the end of the Great War, retired in the mid-1920s. The studio continued to operate under his name until the end of 1927, when Henri Harrison moved in, offering both photographic services and violin lessons. William Berry enjoyed an active, family-filled retirement until 1949, when at the grand age of ninety-two years he passed away.

Berry & Co.'s legacy

In the lead-up to the centenary of the First World War, Te Papa has sought to identify the soldiers and their families in the Berry collection. By putting names to faces, we have been able to research aspects of each soldier's pre- and post-war story, and in some cases reunite the images with direct descendants. While most negatives bear the name of the person who ordered the photographs etched across the top of the plate, the coinciding registers have not survived.[43] The team has drawn on a combination of sources to help identify the soldiers, including information gleaned from the glass plate negatives. The clarity of the digital scans of the plates has enabled a forensic reading of the sitters' uniforms. Unit badges, rank insignia and patches have all provided significant clues, which can be cross-checked with the surname on the plate, the Auckland War Memorial Museum's Cenotaph military database and personnel records held by Archives New Zealand. Direct appeals to the public for help through traditional and social media have also resulted in identifications by family members. With each new piece of information, the faces that gaze at us from the past with such immediacy take on new meaning. As Raphael Samuel writes, the power of pictures 'is the reverse of what they seem. We may think we are going to them for knowledge about the past, but it is the knowledge we bring to them which makes them historically significant, transforming a more or less chance residue of the past into a precious icon.'[44]

Eight of the 82 identified soldiers died in the war. While they all dressed in unifying khaki, visited Berry & Co. and struck similar poses, often with identical backdrops and props, their experiences of the war and its aftermath have proved to be diverse. Together, their stories provide a layered picture of the war as experienced by ordinary New Zealanders who found themselves living, and at times dying, in extraordinary circumstances.

The badges worn by soldiers in the Berry & Co. portraits offer clues to help solve their identities. These examples, from top to bottom, are badges of the New Zealand Army Medical Corps, 5th (Wellington Rifles) Regiment, and the First New Zealand Expeditionary Force (NZEF).

Plates

Note on the text

People depicted in the plates are captioned with their birth and death dates where known. Soldiers are also captioned with their First World War service number and their military rank and unit at the time that the portrait was taken.

George Gordon Campbell Hornig 1912

George Hornig, standing proudly in his brand-new uniform, probably posed for this portrait in 1912, making it one of the earliest surviving soldier portraits taken by the Berry studio.

A decade earlier, George's older brother William Francis Hornig (inset) had his portrait copied in the Berry studio. The original was possibly taken before William departed to fight in the South African (Second Boer) War.

In 1912, George Hornig was a twenty-year-old lieutenant in No. 30 Company (Wellington Technical School) Senior Cadets, which had been formed in 1911, after the introduction of the Territorial Training Scheme. All the boys at the school from fourteen to eighteen years of age drilled on Monday evenings and wore their uniforms at school classes. The company's officers were a little older and had left the school – George was working as a draper in his brother William's shop on Cuba Street, almost opposite the Berry studio. George was apparently an enthusiastic and popular officer in the Cadets.

George volunteered for active service on 13 August 1914, as a sapper (the lowest rank in the Royal New Zealand Engineers, equivalent to an army private) with the Field Engineers. He sailed from Wellington with the Main Body on 13 October and was in action on Gallipoli with the Signalling Troop. On 27 August 1915, while laying a telephone line during an attack on a Turkish trench, he was wounded in the left arm by shrapnel. He was evacuated to Egypt, but was back on the peninsula at the end of October.

Evacuated again to Egypt in December, George appears to have seen out the war there at the New Zealand Base, serving with the Signalling Troop and the Base Kit Stores, and also as a 'motor artificer' (mechanic), between spells in hospital. In December 1918, he sailed for England, where he was discharged from the NZEF on 24 April 1919. On July 28, at Wimbledon, he married Queenie Peel.

Returning to Wellington, the Hornigs set up home in Lyall Bay. George returned to work in his brother's drapery shop and later as a salesman. In his spare time he was an active member of the Legion of Frontiersmen, and from 1942 to 1946 he was back in the army on Home Service. George died at Upper Hutt on 2 April 1983.

George Gordon Campbell Hornig (1892–1983)
Lieutenant, No. 30 Company
(Wellington Technical School) Senior Cadets

Roy Houchen 1914

Born in Wellington on 15 January 1892, Roy Houchen lived with his mother in Constable Street, Newtown, working for a cabinetmaker. Roy had served as a part-time volunteer with the Garrison Artillery since March 1911. He must have been a patriotic young man, as the rather cursory report of his medical inspection in 1914 noted that he had a New Zealand flag tattoed on his right upper arm. Just three days after he attested for service, Roy left Wellington in October with the Main Body of the NZEF, bound for Egypt and the Suez Canal.

Roy's war service was with the Medical Corps, but he was to spend much of his time overseas as a patient himself. Roy served for about two months on Gallipoli from late May, until he was invalided out with diarrhoea. He was sent on to hospital in Malta, where he spent six weeks before he was transported to England and admitted to hospital at Leicester, with a 'debility' for two weeks in late September, then transferred to hospital at Epsom for four weeks. On 24 December 1915 Roy was admitted to hospital with gonorrhoea, and after the 'usual treatment' was reported clear on 14 March 1916. From then until May 1918, Roy went back and forth between active service and a number of periods of hospitalisation. Eventually discharged as no longer fit to serve, he returned to Wellington in February 1919.

In 1921, Roy married Eileen May Lake, daughter of Charles and Jane Lake. The couple lived at 50 Ross Street, Kilbirnie. Six years later, Eileen gave birth to a daughter.

Roy was a member of the Independent Order of Odd Fellows. This global organisation had originated in the United States in 1819 and established a New Zealand branch in 1843; its guiding principle was to provide financial support for fellow brethren in need. Membership of Odd Fellows dwindled through the nineteenth century as governments established public welfare systems. Nonetheless, up until his death Roy belonged to the Loyal William Bain Branch in Kilbirnie.

Roy succumbed to illness on 17 July 1934, aged forty-two, and was buried at Karori Cemetery in Wellington.

Roy Houchen (1892–1934)
Service number 3/172
Private, New Zealand Army Medical Corps

Thomas Henry Mossman, Esther Muriel Mossman and Marion Susan Mossman 1914

Thomas Mossman was a sheep farmer from Waerenga-o-kuri, near Gisborne. At the outbreak of war he was twenty-seven years old, single and a well-known figure in his local community; since 1912 he had been a member of the Gisborne Squadron of the Legion of Frontiersmen.

On 21 October 1914, Thomas became the first of four Mossman brothers to serve in the First World War. The Gisborne Frontiersmen had been selected to fill a shortfall of men in the 2nd Reinforcements of the Otago Mounted Rifles. They left for the training camp at Trentham on 24 October, and the local newspaper reported that 'the men will go into camp in the Legion's uniform'. Thomas is wearing the Legion's uniform in this photograph, which must have been taken some time between his arrival in Wellington and his embarkation on 14 December. The sitting in the Berry studio would have been one of the last times Thomas and his stepmother Marion and sister Esther were together.

Thomas's military service was to be pitifully short. He landed in Egypt on 3 February 1915, but died in Cairo from scarlet fever complications on 12 April. 'Thomas coughed himself to death,' recalls his great-grand-nephew Simon Tate, who goes on to explain how Harry Raynor, a fellow patient, wrote home – bluntly, but honestly – to the Mossman parents with the tragic news.

Tragedy struck the Mossman family again a few weeks later when Thomas's younger brother, James Dilworth Mossman, was killed in action on Gallipoli on 19 May. Two other brothers, William Bertram Mossman and Pynson Wilmott Mossman, survived the war, although Bert, who had been badly wounded in the trenches, found postwar life very difficult. Simon Tate speculates on how it would be have been: 'Thomas and Dilworth and Pynson and Bert all . . . had this immense pressure, that they had a family to come back to, a farm to come back to, and they knew that if they didn't, it would crush [the family].'

Mossman descendants still live on the family property, 'The Laurels', at Waerenga-o-kuri. Laurel leaves are an ancient symbol of remembrance, and every year members of the family add leaves to the Gisborne region's Anzac Day wreaths, plucking them from a hedge that was planted after the war in memory of Thomas and James.

Esther Muriel Mossman (1885–1967)

Thomas Henry Mossman (1887–1915)
Service number 9/728
Gisborne Squadron of the Legion of Frontiersmen

Marion Susan Mossman (1866–1948)

Unidentified soldiers 1914–18

The style of cap worn by 'Oliver' (top left), his brand-new tunic and the lack of any identifying unit insignia suggest that the photograph was taken in the first weeks or even days of the war. There are at least three men with the surname Oliver who enlisted very early in the war and whose descriptions resemble the young man in the photograph: William Henry Oliver, (service number 10/493), Arthur Scott Oliver (service number 8/2458) and George Oliver (service number 10/1941). All three fought in the Gallipoli campaign, and survived it, though they did not all come home. William eventually returned to Feilding in 1919. Arthur was killed in action near Ypres in Belgium in November 1917. George was twice wounded in action on the Western Front but returned to New Zealand and was discharged from the NZEF in March 1919.

'Porter' (top centre) was a gunner in the Royal New Zealand Artillery. Most likely he was one of two single men in their early twenties: Eric Clinton Gordon Porter (service number 2/1951), who was born in 1895 in Wellington and was a cadet on a sheep farm before volunteering for service in March 1915; or Charles Alfred Porter (service number 2/2154), who was born in Auckland in 1893 and departed from Wellington on 13 November 1915 with the 8th Reinforcements. Both Eric and Charles had short periods of military service and survived the war.

Unidentified soldiers, with inscriptions
clockwise from top left

'Oliver' 1914

'Porter' 1915

'Brooks' about 1915

'Armes' 1915–18

'Cotter' 1916–17

'Briggs' 1916–18

William Horace James and Gertrude Miriam James 1915

William James would have sat for these portraits shortly before he left New Zealand for Gallipoli, the first of several decisive engagements in which he fought. The older woman is his mother-in-law, Gertrude. William was working as a clerk for the New Zealand Political Reform League when he enlisted on 6 January 1915. These portraits would have been taken with a special camera that captured six exposures on a single negative.

Born in Australia, William embarked from Wellington with the 4th Reinforcements on 17 April 1915. He fought with the Wellington Infantry Battalion on Gallipoli from 9 June and survived the battle of Chunuk Bair, although he was wounded in the left leg and invalided to Alexandria, Egypt. He later joined the 1st Battalion of what was by then called the Wellington Infantry Regiment in France. He was wounded on 2 October 1916 and was promoted to sergeant on 1 December.

The major battles of 1917 included Messines and Passchendaele, and William fought in both. In September of that year he was promoted to the rank of warrant officer and was the battalion's acting company sergeant major. From 29 June until 10 August 1918, he was detached from the battalion to train with the British Army's elite Guards Division.

William was awarded the Distinguished Conduct Medal for his 'conspicuous gallantry'. The citation stated that between 17 September and 11 November 1918, 'the battalion was engaged on several occasions in heavy fighting, particularly at Briastre on 11 and 12 October when his company suffered severe casualties, and at Le Quesnoy on 4 November 1918 where he did fine reconnaissance work.'

William returned to New Zealand in December 1919 and was discharged from the NZEF in April 1920. He married Ida Elizabeth Anderson in 1922 and took up journalism, working first in Hawera, then in Gisborne for the *Gisborne Herald*. Gertrude died in 1937.

Fighting seems to have been in William's blood, for he re-enlisted in the army in September 1940 as a sergeant. He remained in New Zealand throughout the Second World War, serving with the Hawke's Bay Regiment and as commander of the Guard Company at the Featherston prisoner-of-war camp, finishing the war at the rank of captain. In 1946 he even applied to be sent to Japan on occupation duty with 'J Force', but was rejected because of his age. William died in 1969, aged seventy-four.

William Horace James (1894–1969)
Service number 10/1861
Private, 5th (Wellington) Rifles

Gertrude Miriam James (1866–1937)

Edmund Guthrie Morgan and Francis Harold Morgan, with Joyce Veda 1915

Francis Harold Morgan (right), a sapper in the Royal New Zealand Engineers, and his younger brother Edmund Guthrie Morgan of the 4th Reinforcements were from a large Wellington family. Irish-born John and Scottish-born Christina Morgan had eleven children – six boys and five girls – and three of the boys served in the war. Francis, who enlisted in 1914, was part of the Samoa Advance Party. He reenlisted in 1915, along with Edmund, and both sailed from Wellington on 17 April, destined for Egypt and Gallipoli. This portrait was probably taken shortly before they left.

The young girl, holding a swagger stick topped with a bullet, is Francis and Edmund's niece Joyce. Born in 1912, Joyce was the daughter of Grosvenor William Morgan, Francis and Edmund's elder brother, and his wife, Pearl. Both soldiers named Grosvenor as their next of kin when they enlisted, as their parents had by then passed away. Their older brother Allan, a married tram conductor, embarked with the 32nd Reinforcements in November 1917.

Francis, who before re-enlisting worked as a clerk at the New Zealand Express Company, was the first of the brothers to land at Anzac Cove in June 1915. Edmund followed in July, but his stay was short: after suffering a severe hernia on 27 July, he was invalided back to New Zealand. Edmund was discharged in August 1916 as 'no longer physically fit for active service'. He would die of tuberculosis in Wellington in 1930, aged forty-five.

Francis was also evacuated from Gallipoli on 10 August 1915; in September, he was hospitalised in Malta with dysentery, an extremely common illness at the front. Francis served a full four years and 184 days. When the Second World War broke out, he enlisted for a third time. By then he was forty-eight years old, married and working as a salesman; on account of his age he was placed in the reserves and not mobilised. Francis died on 1 June 1957.

Edmund Guthrie Morgan (1884–1930)
Service number 10/1927
Private, Wellington Infantry Battalion

Joyce Veda Morgan (1912–73)

Francis Harold Morgan (1892–1957)
Service number 4/44
Sapper, Royal New Zealand Engineers

James Arthur Juno 1915

James Juno came from 'the school of hard knocks', according to his grandson Jim. His father, Philip Juneau, a Channel Islander, had come to New Zealand in 1874 with one wife, who then 'disappeared'. Phillip married Mary Thoburn in 1886, and she bore him four surviving sons and a daughter, but by 1900 had 'cleared out'. A blacksmith by trade, Phillip was 'a bit of a scallywag', tending to neglect his children in favour of horse-racing. James and his brother Frederick got into petty thieving and were sent to Burnham, a school for delinquents. When war broke out, all four Juno boys were quick to sign up. James enlisted in the Wellington Infantry Battalion on 15 February 1915, citing five years' cadet service on his attestation form. At the time, he was working as a farmhand. He probably posed for this photograph shortly before going overseas on 13 June.

James arrived on Gallipoli on 11 August, three days after the death of his older brother, George, on Chunuk Bair. James was to remain in action on Gallipoli with the Wellington Infantry Battalion until the evacuation to Egypt in late December. On 6 April 1916, he embarked for France with the 1st Battalion of what was by then the Wellington Infantry Regiment; there he served in the front line from 3 August until his departure on 4 December 1917 for leave in England. He was admitted to hospital three weeks later and spent most of the next five months in English hospitals with a number of ailments including gastritis, finally leaving for home on 30 May 1918. He arrived in New Zealand on 6 August and was discharged on 12 December.

Under the Discharged Soldiers Settlement Act 1915, the New Zealand Government purchased land for returning soldiers in order to help them resettle and develop farms. The sections of farmland were allocated by ballot and in 1919, James won a ballot for land for his own dairy farm at the Pihautea Returned Soldiers' Settlement near Featherston.

James married Florence Willoughby in 1920, and they had four children. He became closely involved in the local community; he served on the dairy board for many years, helped build the local hall, and assisted with the rifle and tennis clubs. But, recalls Jim, he was a tough man, nicknamed 'the colonel' by his children. Florence died in 1943, and James died at Featherston on 14 June 1954.

James Arthur Juno (1891–1954)
Service number 10/2194
Private, Wellington Infantry Battalion

John William Kaywood 1915

John Kaywood volunteered for service and enlisted at Trentham Camp on 19 April 1915. At the time, he was working as a plumber in Wellington for Taylor, Ramsey and Co. There is a discrepancy over his age: his enlistment records state his age as being twenty-four years and four months, but according to his death certificate he would have been almost a year younger. Early in the war, young men keen to fight often added months or even years to their age, in order to be eligible to serve. In John's case, it may have simply been a mistake, as he was over twenty-one anyway.

On 13 June 1915, John embarked from Wellington as a gunner with the 5th Reinforcements, bound for Egypt. Gunners played a hugely important role in the First World War, working in teams on field guns, usually grouped in batteries, to deliver a concentrated barrage. It was a dangerous and demanding job. Not only were they being targeted by enemy batteries, the work was physically punishing and they were also at risk of shells exploding in the barrels of the guns.

John was on active service with the Field Artillery on Gallipoli from 13 August 1915 until his evacuation and return to Egypt on 22 December. He left Egypt again with his unit on 7 April 1916 for service on the Western Front, but was wounded in February 1917.

In October 1918, just weeks before the Armistice, John was promoted to bombardier. In March 1919, John sailed from Liverpool for home; he had served for a total of four years and fifty days, having spent just eighty-five of those days in New Zealand and the remainder overseas.

John married Olive Mary Ambridge at Auckland on 27 December 1920. He passed away in 1972 at the age of eighty-one, and Olive lived to be ninety-eight years old. They are buried at Kelvin Grove Cemetery in Palmerston North.

John William Kaywood (1891–1972)
Service number 2/1799
Gunner, New Zealand Field Artillery

Cecil Charles Baker
and Hannah Irene Baker 1915

Cecil Baker had almost finished his military training when he married Hannah Harvey at the Kent Terrace Presbyterian Church in Wellington on 22 July 1915. A few weeks after this wedding portrait, he left New Zealand with the 6th Reinforcements.

Cecil should never have been accepted for military service. He had been working as a bushman near Collingwood when he enlisted on 17 April 1915. He was rejected as 'unfit for war service' because the large toe of his right foot had been amputated following a bicycle accident when he was thirteen or fourteen years old. This would have left him unable to march long distances. After 'repeated rejections', however, he was eventually accepted in August 1915 without an inspection of his feet.

The army found him useful employment as a cook, and he spent seven weeks with the Canterbury Infantry Battalion on Gallipoli prior to the evacuation in December 1915. He was hospitalised in Egypt for much of early 1916, suffering from gastritis, catarrh and jaundice; after briefly rejoining his unit in mid-February, he was readmitted to hospital with a 'painful inflammation' of the stump of his amputated toe. Cecil spent the remainder of his military career as a cook at New Zealand military hospitals in England, except for two periods in July–August of 1917 and 1918, when he was granted 'agricultural leave' to help with the harvest on nearby farms. In February 1918, a medical board recommended that he be declared 'permanently unfit for war service, fit for base duties', and he was eventually discharged from the NZEF in New Zealand on 18 April 1919.

Cecil and Hannah divorced in 1927 in Westport, where he continued to live until his death in 1965.

Cecil Charles Baker (1890–1965)
Service number 6/2532
Private, 6th Reinforcements

Hannah Irene Baker, née Harvey (1896–unknown)

Middleton Beckett and Helen Mary Beckett 1915

Middleton Beckett, photographed with his sister, Helen, was born at Norsewood on 17 August 1896 and educated at Wanganui Collegiate. He first worked as a clerk with the Bank of New South Wales in Napier, later transferring to its Christchurch branch. Keen to join up, he volunteered at the outbreak of war, but was rejected as being too young. In May 1915 he tried again, falsifying his age by two years, and was enlisted in the newly formed Rifle Brigade.

Middleton was assigned to the brigade's 2nd Battalion and trained at a new camp at Rangiotu in the Manawatu. The brigade had not yet been issued with metal cap and collar badges, and the temporary distinguishing badge of each battalion was a piece of black cloth on the hat – a diamond for the 1st and a rectangle for the 2nd. The patch shows clearly on Middleton's service cap and, since metal badges were not issued to the Rifle Brigade prior to 31 August, his visit to the Berry studio can be dated to a week's leave from 20–27 August.

The 2nd Battalion sailed from Wellington on 9 October, later that year fighting pro-Turkish Senussi tribesmen in Egypt's Western Desert. But the battalion was to face a much more sophisticated enemy when it was sent to France in April 1916 to fight against Germany.

On the night of 26 May, Middleton was on a night patrol near Armentières, laying barbed wire in front of the brigade's trenches, when a shell fragment struck him in the back. He was taken to a casualty clearing station, but died of his wounds two days later and was buried at Bailleul. He was not yet twenty. Middleton was one of the first Rifle Brigade men to die on the Western Front.

The photograph of Middleton with his sister is perhaps the most poignant of the three portraits taken at the sitting. Helen was two years younger than him and, like him, was to die far too young. She never married. She trained as a nurse and from 1930 worked for the Plunket Society as their district nurse in the Wellington suburbs of Island Bay, Berhampore and Newtown. Working among struggling families in the worst years of the Depression, Helen won a reputation for selfless service, and her sudden death at the age of thirty-eight was deeply mourned in the community.

Helen Mary Beckett (1894–1932)

Middleton Beckett (1896–1916)
Service number 24/971
Rifleman, 2nd Battalion, New Zealand Rifle Brigade

William Charles Bevan 1915

When he attested for military service in June 1915, William Bevan was twenty-nine years old and had been working as a labourer in the Wellington region. He gave his next of kin as his sister, Lily Urquhart, who lived on Thorndon Quay.

William embarked from Wellington on 9 October 1915, bound for Egypt with the New Zealand Veterinary Corps. On 17 April 1916, however, he was transferred to the Field Artillery to serve as a gunner. After training in England, he was posted to France on 17 October 1916, where he joined the 13th Battery, New Zealand Divisional Artillery. William was wounded in action in June 1917.

Once he had recovered, William rejoined his unit in France and worked as a driver of the teams of horses used to pull guns. In March 1918, however, he was kicked in the abdomen by a horse and was seriously injured, with a ruptured small intestine and internal haemorrhaging. After undergoing surgery at Bethnal Green Hospital in London, he was sent to the hospital at Brockenhurst to recover. However, he was found unfit by the medical board and returned to New Zealand in August 1918.

William Charles Bevan (1886–unknown)
Service number 17/336
Trooper, 7th Reinforcements,
New Zealand Veterinary Corps

John Owen Clay 1915

Born in Melbourne, Australia, railway worker John Clay was twenty-eight years old when he attested for military service on 23 August 1915 at Trentham. In this photograph he wears the uniform of a trooper in the Mounted Rifles.

John was first posted to the 8th Mounted Rifles, transferring on 28 November to the 11th Mounted Rifles. He was promoted to corporal on 2 December and to sergeant on 20 January 1916. His active war service was not, however, to be with the cavalry. He embarked on 1 April 1916 with the 11th Reinforcements, and on arrival in Egypt was posted to the 1st Battalion, Canterbury Infantry Regiment as a private.

John was sent with his regiment to France, where he fought in the Battle of the Somme. This was New Zealand's first major engagement on the Western Front, beginning with an advance across no man's land on 15 September. The New Zealand Division fought for 19 consecutive days and suffered nearly 5500 wounded and over 1500 killed – all for an advance of some eight kilometres. John himself was seriously injured on 25 September. His military medical report, which describes it as a 'compound fracture of the skull', gives a dry account: 'While in a bayonet charge he was struck by a bullet, sustaining an extensive depression over posterior frontal region.' After a period of recovery he was discharged from service in April 1917.

John lived in the Wellington area after the war. In 1933 he married Bridget Firth, owner of the Western Park Hotel in Wellington; John appears to have worked in the hotel, and as a railway worker, until retiring in 1946. John and Bridget's son, also named John Owen Clay, remembered the scar on his father's head from his injury in the war. 'He had a dent, in the top of his head. If he held his head up, he could keep about a tablespoon of water in it. And that was it; we just never questioned it.'

John died at Silverstream Hospital in the Hutt Valley in July 1968, aged eighty-one.

John Owen Clay (1887–1968)
Service number 10133
Trooper, Mounted Rifles

Edmund Colin Nigel Robinson and Mary Theresa Veronica Robinson 1915

Edmund Robinson, one of the few officers in the Berry collection, married Mary Read on 11 September 1915, and this is their wedding portrait. In keeping with wartime, Mary wore a navy blue military-style dress, as the *Dominion* reported, but also a 'French hat of pale pink and blue, trimmed with roses'.

Edmund was twenty-four years old when he attested for service in 1915. He had been working as a farmer at Pihama, Taranaki, but came originally from Croydon in London. Edmund embarked for Europe on 13 November 1915, attached to the 2nd Reinforcements and posted to the 1st Battalion, New Zealand Rifle Brigade. In June 1917, he was gassed during the Allied offensive at Messines. He suffered a severe cough and would later be diagnosed with chronic lung disease; nonetheless, after returning to New Zealand he lived a relatively long life.

After the war Edmund applied for, and won, some land in a ballot. He farmed at Mangateparu, Morrinsville, for the rest of his life. In October 1940, he was appointed as the Paeroa area commander for the Home Guard, New Zealand's home defence force during the Second World War. He was also a prominent member of the Returned Services' Association.

Mary was the first of three women who were married to Edmund. She died in 1959. Edmund married Margaret Morrison in 1961 and, after a divorce, Jean Alexander in 1967. He had three children. Edmund died in 1972 aged eighty-two.

Edmund Colin Nigel Robinson (1890–1972)
Service number 23/1303
Lieutenant, 2nd Reinforcements, 1st Battalion,
New Zealand Rifle Brigade

Mary Theresa Veronica Robinson, née Read (unknown–1959)

Unidentified soldiers 1916–18

The soldier at top left is one of seven 'Harris' images in the wider Berry collection, including a portrait of an older woman and portraits of two young girls in uniform, one of whom (see page 7) stands to attention and gives the three-fingered salute of the Girl Peace Scouts. She may be the soldier's daughter or relative.

We can see from the insignia on his uniform that 'Murray' (top centre) was a gunner in the Royal New Zealand Artillery. His hat badge features a cannon, while his collar badges take the form of old-fashioned artillery shells. He also wears a bandolier, indicating that he may have been the driver of a team of horses, which pulled guns and ammunition wagons. A pocketed belt for carrying ammunition, bandoliers were designed to be worn fastened over the shoulder, in order to keep the weight of the ammunition off the hips and allow easy access to the ammunition for soldiers on horseback. This particular style was introduced in 1916 .

'Wilcox' (bottom right) is quite likely to be Robert Wilcox (service number 54720), born 26 June 1892, who was a farmer living in Buckland, near Pukekohe, serving with the Waikato Regiment. Enlisting voluntarily for overseas service in Auckland on 15 February 1917, he embarked from Wellington with the 30th Reinforcements on 13 October. While serving in France, Robert ripped his left hand open on barbed wire in front of a trench, an injury that would become a permanent disability; he could 'make a good fist', but his grip was poor. After discharge from the NZEF on 21 January 1919, Robert returned to the Buckland community and died in 1994, at the age of ninety-four.

Their collar insignia, featuring the serpent-entwined Rod of Asclepius, mark both 'Henderson' (lower left) and the unidentified soldier at lower centre as members of the New Zealand Army Medical Corps. Beyond that, however, their identities remain a mystery. A great number of Hendersons served in the Medical Corps during the First World War, most famously Richard Alexander 'Dick' Henderson, awarded the Military Medal for rescuing the injured at the Somme. One potential candidate for the soldier at lower right is John Christie Henderson (serial number 3/2902) of Christchurch, a private who sailed with the hospital ship *Marama* in March 1917 and January 1918.

Degradation in the emulsion has erased the inscription on the glass plate negative for the lower centre portrait. As such the surname of the soldier depicted is unknown, but his uniform and badges, including the star on his right sleeve, show that he was a quartermaster-sergeant. He would have been responsible for the administration of medical supplies in a military hospital.

Unidentified soldiers, with inscriptions *clockwise from top left*

'Harris' 1916–19

'Murray' about 1917

'Parks' about 1917

'Wilcox' 1916–18

no inscription. about 1918

'Henderson', 1917–18

William Henry Bates 1915

William Bates was born in Eastbourne, England, in 1889. When he attested for service in 1915, he was twenty-six years old, working in Wellington as a draper's assistant, and his parents were still living in England.

William joined a field ambulance unit of the New Zealand Army Medical Corps. He trained at the Awapuni Camp in Palmerston North. While the camps at Trentham and Featherston were established to convert 'citizens into fighting men', the Awapuni Camp was for the 'efficient training of men who have chosen for their "little bit" in the war the care and succour of comrades' – that is, the Medical Corps. At Awapuni the recruits were taught everything from squad and camp drill to clerical work, including how to inventory the possessions of the wounded, as well as the particulars of first aid during warfare.

William's file records that he was charged with the offence of arriving late at Trentham Camp on 30 October; nonetheless he embarked for Alexandria on New Zealand Hospital Ship No. 2 *Marama*, which sailed from Wellington on 5 December 1915. The hospital ships *Marama* and *Maheno*, acquired by the New Zealand Government and equipped by public donations, made several voyages between 1915 and 1919, primarily to ferry the wounded from the Western Front and Mediterranean–Aegean theatre to hospital in England or Egypt.

In December 1917, William was discharged from service on grounds that he was no longer physically fit. A medical board that had examined him on 5 December diagnosed hypochondriasis, which today is more commonly termed 'health anxiety'. In Williams' case the board considered it to have been a pre-existing condition aggravated by wartime service. At the time of his discharge he was a patient at Waikato Sanatorium, near Cambridge.

William's health fears would appear to have been misplaced, for he enjoyed a long life. After the war he moved to Whanganui and died in 1975.

William Henry Bates (1889–1975)
Service number 3/1368
Private, New Zealand Medical Corps

Herbert Costello, William Costello and Frederick Costello 1915–16

Two of the three Costello brothers, (from left to right) Herbert, William and Frederick, served in the NZEF during the war.

Born in 1882, Herbert was thirty-two years old when he enlisted in the NZEF. Prior to this he was self-employed as a bushman. Assigned to the Canterbury Infantry Battalion, he went to Trentham Camp in December 1915. His service record betrays something of a disregard for rules, listing three separate infringements of overstaying leave.

Herbert was among the New Zealand casualties at Passchendaele (845 died and about 2700 were wounded) on 12 October 1917, the worst day for New Zealand during the war, when the troops made a failed attack against strongly held German defences on a ridge called Bellevue Spur. Hit in the left forearm by machine-gun fire, Herbert was hospitalised in England; eventually he returned home, unfit for service, on the *Maunganui* in March 1918. Herbert spent the rest of his life in Wellington and died in 1950.

William Costello was recorded as the next of kin for both of his brothers. He had cared for them since the early deaths of their parents, Matthew and Mildred, and when Herbert and Frederick went away to war he provided a 'home base'. In 1898, William married Phoebe Olive Wilton, youngest daughter of Elijah and Priscilla Wilton (the Wilton family donated Wilton's Bush to the city of Wellington). William and Phoebe had ten children and lived in Douro Avenue in Newtown, Wellington. Phoebe died in September 1940, and William passed away in Whanganui in 1943. They are buried in Karori Cemetery.

The third brother, Frederick, had worked as a tailor for a Mr Hackett in Te Kuiti prior to the war. When he enlisted in 1915, he used a false birth date (23 July 1880) to ensure he was not too old for overseas service. He was assigned to the New Zealand Rifle Brigade with the 4th Battalion, and in this portrait he wears the Brigade's collar and hat badges, featuring a lion holding a pennant. The blaze of black cloth on his cap – a triangle with point down – confirms the 4th Battalion. Frederick embarked for Suez on February 1916. After training, he was posted in April 1916 to France, where he served at the front for the remainder of the war. He sailed from Liverpool on the *Northumberland*, arriving home to be officially discharged on 28 March 1919. Frederick lived in Napier until his death on 4 May 1942.

Herbert Lenton Costello (1882–1950)
Service number 6/4596
Private, Canterbury Infantry Battalion

William Costello (1875–1943)

Frederick Costello (1878–1942)
Service number 26/741
Private, 4th Battalion, New Zealand Rifle Brigade

William Keith Berry 1916

Keith Berry, born in Kaikoura, was twenty-one years old when he attested for service in October 1915. He was living in Napier at the time, working as a telegraphist for the New Zealand Post Office. He embarked for Egypt on 5 February 1916; assigned to the New Zealand Rifle Brigade, he went to France and fought at the Somme.

Keith's military record reveals how he was punished twice: once for being absent without leave, and later for 'hesitating to put on his gas mask'. It seems likely that he was slow to put on his mask during training at Armentières and his superiors made an example of him; committing the same error at the front line would have been fatal. He was given Field Punishment No. 2 – marching for many hours each day in full kit – and tasked with scrubbing floors and other chores.

But Keith was also rewarded, gaining promotion to lance corporal, and later corporal and then sergeant. On 15 September 1916, he received a shrapnel wound in the left knee and was evacuated to the hospital at Walton-on-Thames; he was also treated there for recurrent influenza in May 1918. By this time he had been transferred to the Medical Corps and was working at the hospital, probably in administrative posts. He evidently worked hard, given that he received the Meritorious Service Medal for his work at the hospital, and it was there that his met his future wife.

Keith Berry married Louise, a military hospital nurse, on 9 July 1919 in Maidstone, Kent. Returning to New Zealand after the war, they had two children, Zoe (who died at birth) and Allan. Keith worked for the New Zealand Post Office all his working life, initially as a telegraphist in Napier, and later as postmaster in Otaki, Te Puke and Ohakune. During the Second World War, he took it on himself to hand-deliver the dreaded telegrams bearing bad news of the killed, wounded or missing. 'When he went down the street,' recalls Allan, 'women would be howling, hoping that he would not be stopping at their house with this awful telegram, with its news.'

Keith died on 21 January 1962, aged sixty-six, in Otorohanga. Allan recalls how, over the years, his father had had a lot of pain from his old war wound. 'They didn't remove the shrapnel because they thought it would be more dangerous to remove it . . . so he died with the shrapnel still in his knee.'

William Keith Berry (1894–1962)
Service number 25/81
Rifleman, 3rd Battalion,
New Zealand Rifle Brigade

Percy Alfred Vincent 1916

Percy Vincent was forty-one years old when he enlisted on 9 January 1916. A veteran of the South African (Second Boer) War, he was working at the time as a labourer for the Public Works Department at Gisborne. He embarked for overseas service with the 12th Reinforcements on 6 May. At the time he left, Percy was single and had listed his sister, Helen Humphreys of Brighton, England, as his next of kin.

Percy spent two years on the Western Front, serving from 23 September 1916 until 26 August 1918. He was hospitalised in October 1917 with a condition known as ICT (inflammation of connective tissue) on his right hand, and again in July 1918 suffering from myalgia (muscle pain arising from strain or injury). When he returned to New Zealand and was discharged from the NZEF in January 1919, a note on his file stated that he was 'no longer fit for war service' and 'prematurely aged', with an atrophied right arm.

Despite this, Percy appears to have continued working as a labourer in the postwar years. By 1946 he had retired, and he died aged seventy-three at Auckland Hospital on 10 September 1948.

Percy Alfred Vincent (1875–1948)
Service number 12516
Private, 2nd Battalion,
Wellington Infantry Regiment

Sidney Cresswell 1916

Sidney Cresswell was aged twenty-six, single and working as a wire mattress maker in Wellington when he volunteered for the Army Service Corps in December 1915. Since there were too many volunteers for the corps from Wellington, he was one of several men who were asked at a special parade on 8 December if they were prepared to transfer to other units. Sidney agreed to join the Mounted Rifles and enlisted with the 12th Reinforcements on 11 January 1916. He was posted immediately to train with them at Tauherinikau Camp near Featherston. He was with the Mounted Rifles until 5 April, when he was transferred to the infantry.

Sidney embarked from Wellington with the 12th Reinforcements on 6 May 1916. He arrived in England via Egypt on 7 August for training at Sling Camp, but fell sick and was admitted to Tidworth Military Hospital in Wiltshire on 24 August. On his recovery in October, he was transferred to NZEF Group Headquarters as a groom, then to the Pioneer Battalion at Sling. Sent to France on 30 October, he served with the battalion until 25 February 1917, when he was detached for duty with the 1st British Army's Forest Control unit. In May, Sidney was permanently attached to one of the Royal Engineers forestry companies. Forestry work was crucial in supporting fighting troops, as huge amounts of timber was needed to make 'duckboards' (walkways across sodden ground) and other constructions. Sidney had brief periods of leave in England in June–July 1917 and February 1918, then served with the forestry company until the end of the year.

Sidney was at Larkhill Camp in Wiltshire when he fell sick with influenza. He was admitted to the nearby Fargo Military Hospital on 4 February 1919, then to the New Zealand Convalescent Hospital at Hornchurch. A medical board examined him on 20 February and recommended he be classified as 'B3' (unfit for war service) for three months. Departing for New Zealand on 11 March, Sidney was examined during the voyage by another medical board, which, although it attributed his 'debility' to war service, recommended that he not be given a disability pension. He was discharged from the NZEF at Wellington on 27 May 1919.

On 24 March 1921, Sidney married Lillian Rose Edwards, whom he may have met in England, but who died only two years later. He remarried in 1924, to Amy Sarah Hurley, and lived to the age of eighty-three.

Sidney Cresswell (1888–1971)
Service number 10325
Trooper, 12th Reinforcements,
New Zealand Pioneer Battalion

Pryce Roberts 1916

Pryce Roberts was born in North Wales on 12 December 1875. At the time of his enlistment in the NZEF on 16 February 1916 he was a single man, working as a carpenter at Manaia, Taranaki. He joined the Royal New Zealand Engineers as a sapper, and it was in that uniform that he sat for his portrait prior to embarking for overseas service on 21 May.

Pryce was not to see active service on the Western Front, as he remained in England due to a knee injury, serving as a cook for the Engineers and as a tradesman for the New Zealand Hospital at Brockenhurst. On 21 March 1917, he married Annie Vaughan Lloyd. Pryce was finally declared medically unfit on 10 October 1918 and returned to New Zealand. He and his wife clearly returned to Britain some time after the war, given that in 1950 he applied from an English address to the Defence Department in Wellington for his service medals. Since he had not been on 'active service in a theatre of war', the department informed him that he was eligible only for the British War Medal and not the Victory Medal.

Pryce Roberts (1875–unknown)
Service number 23728
Sapper, Royal New Zealand Engineers

Gordon Grant Sutherland 1916

When he enlisted for military service at Featherston on 10 March 1916, Gordon Sutherland was twenty years old and had been working as a butcher in his home town of Duntroon, South Canterbury. He named his father, William Sutherland, as next of kin. Gordon was posted the next day to the Army Service Corps as a driver. He embarked from Wellington for overseas service with the 14th Reinforcements on 26 June 1916, bound for England.

After training at Sling Camp, Gordon joined the Army Service Corps in France on 16 November. Gordon's duties involved driving horse- or mule-drawn wagons carrying ammunition, food and other supplies, often under enemy shellfire and aerial bombardment. He would also have had to care for the animals in his teams. On 15 October 1917, possibly as a respite from this duty, he was transferred to the divisional horse-clipping depot, where he stayed till 11 December. Many thousands of horses and mules were used on the Western Front, and their coats needed regular clipping to help prevent skin infection. Gordon spent a second spell at the depot in February 1918, after which he joined Headquarters Company of the Army Service Corps. He had a spell of leave in England in October 1918. He embarked from Liverpool on the *Maunganui* on 17 May 1919, arrived back in New Zealand on 24 June and was discharged from the NZEF on 21 July.

Gordon endured three European winters during his military service, which may account for his application only six weeks after his discharge for medical treatment at the expense of the Defence Department. He complained of pain in his ankle, knee and hip joints and was diagnosed as suffering from 'chronic articular rheumatism'. The examining medical officer recommended that Gordon be treated at the thermal baths at Rotorua, but this pleasurable therapy was not to be; instead, his superior allocated Gordon to Oamaru Hospital as an outpatient.

After the war Gordon married Bessie Jane Parker from Millers Flat in 1927, with whom he had one child, Jean Isabell. He died at Oamaru on 21 April 1947, aged only fifty-one; Bessie outlived him by more than thirty years, passing away on 27 May 1978.

Gordon Grant Sutherland (1896–1947)
Service number 16180
Driver, New Zealand Army Service Corps

William George Roberts 1916

William Roberts was born at Petone on 24 October 1895. When he enlisted in May 1916, he was living with his mother at 8 Hopper Street, Wellington, a short walk away from Berry & Co.'s studio, and working as a typewriter mechanic for the Remington & Roneo Agency.

William trained at Trentham with the 16th Reinforcements. This photograph was probably taken shortly before he embarked for England on 19 August. Arriving at Sling Camp on 26 October, he was posted to the Rifle Brigade's 5th Reserve Battalion. He left for France on 15 November and served with the Rifle Brigade's 3rd Battalion from 7 December 1916 to 6 August 1917, when he was detached for 20 days to the 2nd Field Company of the Royal New Zealand Engineers. William had leave periods in the United Kingdom late in 1917 and in Paris early in 1918 and he was promoted to lance corporal on 28 March.

On 21 April, William was admitted to hospital for what his file describes as 'ICT [inflammation of connective tissue] chest wall', which may refer to pleurisy. He rejoined his unit eight days later, but on 3 May was back for a day to be treated for boils on his back. On 30 June he relinquished his rank of lance corporal at his own request.

More hospital spells were to come. Shot in the neck on 1 August 1918, William was taken to a Canadian hospital at Doullens in northern France. After a series of hospital transfers, he went on leave to the United Kingdom in October, rejoining his unit on 5 November. William left England for New Zealand on 12 April 1919 and was discharged from the NZEF on 27 June, returning to his mother's home and his job as a typewriter mechanic.

On 22 February 1921, at Brooklyn, Wellington, William married Fanny Barbara Hazel Cook. When he re-enlisted in the army on 2 July 1940 for service with the infantry in the Second World War, he was living in the suburb of Ngaio and still working as a typewriter mechanic. He served with the army in New Zealand until his discharge on 11 May 1942. William died in Wellington on 18 May 1964.

William George Roberts (1895–1964)
Service number 20236
Private, 16th Reinforcements

John Edgar Vaughan 1916

Born in 1896 at Waimea South, Nelson, John Vaughan had been working as a farmer and was unmarried when he enlisted for military service in 1916. He listed his father, AH Vaughan of Waitapu, Takaka, as his next of kin. He embarked on 19 January 1917 from Wellington aboard the *Ulimaroa*, bound for Plymouth.

John fought in the Third Battle of Ypres, known as Passchendaele. On 16 October 1917, he was wounded and severely gassed. Later, he contracted diphtheria, and on 24 October 1917 was hospitalised at Brockenhurst in England. He was transferred to the Convalescent Depot in Hornchurch on 15 January 1918.

The photograph shows John wearing the single chevron of a lance corporal. By the end of the war, however, he had been promoted to sergeant.

After the war, John lived at Waitapu, near Takaka, Golden Bay. He lived in the Takaka area all his life, serving as a Justice of the Peace. He was married three times and had one son to his first wife, Gladys Irene Rose, whom he married in 1926 at St Andrew's Presbyterian Church in Takaka. It was rare for veterans of the war to live into their ninth decade, especially those who had suffered the trauma of poison gas, but John was one of these few who beat the odds. John died in 1987, aged ninety, and was survived by his son and seven grandchildren.

John Edgar Vaughan (1896–1987)
Service number 26344
Lance corporal, 17th Reinforcements

Unidentified couples 1916–18

The Howes (top left) ordered three cabinet prints of their portrait. The unknown private wears a 'lemon-squeezer' hat and holds an ebony 'swagger stick', which features two silver-plated cartridges at the top and may have been commissioned from a local jeweller. Carried off-duty, the swagger stick has often been viewed as an affectation, although the *Auckland Star* reported that it played a crucial part in the training of Canadian soldiers: it prevented them from putting their right hand in their trouser pocket – something a 'finished soldier' would never do.

Over 300 men with the surname 'Green' served New Zealand in the First World War. Unfortunately, there are no badges on this man's uniform (lower right) to help identify his unit, and the couple's identity remains unknown. When cropped, the background in this photograph would create the impression they were standing in front of a wall with decorative carved panelling.

The Watts (lower centre) are likely to be Charles Grant Watt (service number 3/3842) of Wellington and his wife Elizabeth. Under the rather judgemental headline 'Unwilling Recruits', the *Dominion* reported on 16 May 1917 that Charles, who owned a watchmaking and jewellery business in Manners Street, Wellington, was 'granted a suspension for two months in order that he might have an opportunity of disposing of his business'. Seven months later, in December 1917, Charles departed for the war as a private in the 33rd Reinforcements of the New Zealand Medical Corps. If this portrait is of Charles and Elizabeth, it was taken before he was issued with his Medical Corp badges. Another possibility is that the sitters are John Alexander Watt (service number 81056) of Masterton and his wife Margaret, but as John had auburn hair and stood just 5 feet 4 inches (1.62 metres) tall, they are less likely to be the sitters.

Berry & Co., like most studios of the time, used dry plate negatives; these were coated with a gelatin-based emulsion, which held the light-sensitive materials that captured the light to create the image. Unfortunately, the emulsion layer of the glass plate negative for the unknown couple (at top right) has suffered significant degradation. The soldier wears a generic NZEF cap and collar badges.

Unidentified soldiers and women, with inscriptions
clockwise from top left

'Howe' 1915–18

'Callum' 1915–8

no insciription 1915–18

'Bolton' 1917–18

'Watt' 1917–18

'Green' 1917–18

Ashley Heath Baigent and Annie Baigent 1917

Ashley Baigent strikes a confident pose with a bandolier over his left shoulder and riding spurs on his boots, but his war service was to be brief and uneventful. A farmer from Takaka, Golden Bay, at the time he attested for service on 8 January 1917, he was assigned to the New Zealand Field Artillery's 25th Reinforcements, but was found to have a goitre and therefore 'unfit for active service'. Standing at Ashley's side is his wife, Annie. She was born in 1892 to Reuben and Mary Packard of Motupipi, near Takaka, and married Ashley in 1917.

After the war Ashley became the director of the Nelson Freezing Works and for many years worked as a fatstock buyer. He also served as a county councillor and a member of the Takaka Show Committee. He took over his father's farm in the 1940s in partnership with his brother Phillip. Ashley Baigent died on 17 May 1958; Annie passed away on 19 August 1976 at the age of eighty-four.

Annie Baigent, née Packard (1892–1976)

Ashley Heath Baigent (1890–1958)
Service number 42970
Gunner, 25th Reinforcements,
New Zealand Field Artillery

John Frederick Taylor and Maud Florence Taylor 1917

This striking wedding portrait shows John and Maud Taylor, who were married on 15 February 1917. John wears spurs, a bandolier and an ammunition pouch, indicating he was a member of the mounted rifles, as well as the distinctive 'double horse' collar and hat badges worn by the 23rd and 24th Mounted Rifles Reinforcements.

Born in Waterloo, Sydney, John Taylor was twenty-two years old and working for the Jerseydale Cheese Factory, Eltham, when he enlisted in the 23rd Mounted Reinforcements on 3 October 1916. His parents, Joseph and Sarah, had originally emigrated from England, arriving in New Zealand in 1903.

John had served twenty months as a territorial in the 5th Wellington Regiment prior to his war service. In February 1917, while he was training at Trentham, he was granted leave for his wedding. This was a second marriage for Maud, then a thirty-four-year-old widow, who had married her first husband, Angus McLeod, in 1902 and borne four children. On marrying Maud, John became their stepfather. Later the same year, while John was on overseas service, Maud gave birth to his own son, Francis John Frederick.

In June 1917, John arrived in Suez, Egypt. Posted initially to the New Zealand Veterinary Corps, he was later transferred to the New Zealand Mounted Rifles Brigade. The Mounted Rifles were engaged in a campaign against Turkish forces in Palestine during 1917–18. While in the field in September 1918, John was admitted to hospital. There is no specific cause listed, but it was serious enough that he was invalided back to New Zealand, leaving Egypt in December on the *Malta*.

It was at sea that John contracted pneumonic influenza. When the ship arrived in Perth, Western Australia, he was removed and placed in quarantine. By then he had serious pneumonia and was very sick indeed: over a six-day period from 6 January 1919, his temperature hovered in the range of 38.3–40.6°C. He recovered, however, and returned to New Zealand in April 1919. In December, he was discharged 'in consequence of being no longer physically fit for war service on account of illness contracted while on active service'.

John Taylor died in Stratford, Taranaki, on 20 November 1971; Maud had passed away twenty years earlier in Eltham. They are buried together in Hawera Cemetery.

John Frederick Taylor (1895–1971)
Service number 35851
Trooper, 23rd Reinforcements,
New Zealand Mounted Rifles

Maud Florence Taylor, née Des Forges (1883–1951)

Thomas Fleming Stewart 1917

Born in Scotland on 24 December 1888, Thomas Stewart emigrated to New Zealand in about 1910. His parents, James and Robina Stewart, followed a year later, settling in Lepperton, a small town in the Taranaki region; Thomas listed his father as his next of kin. At the time of his enlistment in the NZEF on 27 October 1916 Thomas was twenty-seven years old, working as a farm labourer for a Mr Holmes at Tiraumea, near Eketahuna.

Thomas trained with the 23rd Reinforcements and posed for another portrait (inset) with two other soldiers from the same unit, one of whom (right) could be Francis Beaufort (see page 72). The other soldier (seated) is unidentified. The 23rd Reinforcements embarked from Wellington on 14 March 1917, bound for England. When Thomas marched into Sling Camp on 21 May for further training, he was posted to the 4th Reserve Battalion of the Auckland-Wellington Regiment. Exactly one month later, he was sent to France on active service. He was at the Base Depot at Étaples from 23 June till 9 July, when he went to the front to join the 3rd Battalion, Wellington Infantry Regiment.

Thomas's time in the front line was tragically brief: he was killed in action the following day. He was buried at Motor Car Corner Military Cemetery in Belgium, south-east of Ploegsteert, near the French border. The cemetery was so named because it marked the point beyond which military cars were not permitted to proceed towards the front. Thomas's body lies there today along with those of eighty other New Zealanders.

Thomas Fleming Stewart (1888–1917)
Service number 39909
Private, 23rd Reinforcements,
Wellington Infantry Regiment

Francis Edward Beaufort 1917

Francis Beaufort was twenty-nine years old when he attested for military service on 23 October 1916. At the time he lived in Pahiatua and worked as a storeman for the Wairarapa Farmers' Co-operative Association.

Francis entered training camp on 2 January 1917 and embarked from Wellington for England with the 23rd Reinforcements on 14 March, disembarking at Devonport, England, on 21 May. After training at Sling Camp in Wiltshire, Francis was sent to France on 22 June. He joined the 1st Battalion, Wellington Infantry Regiment and fought with them at Passchendaele, New Zealand's bloodiest engagement of the war. To have survived the shelling and gas attacks he must have been either tough or lucky, or both – but he clearly also served with distinction, for on 31 October, he was awarded the Military Medal for his gallantry in that battle.

In March 1918, Francis was wounded in the left shoulder and transported to hospital in England – first Walton-on-Thames, and later Hornchurch. He returned to New Zealand on 23 June 1919.

On 31 March 1920, at the Presbyterian Church in Carterton, Francis married Margaret Sutherland Grant. The Beauforts and Grants were both well-known families and it was a big society wedding. Francis died on 26 June 1930, aged only forty-three. His son, Digby James Beaufort, served in Italy with the 25th Infantry Battalion during the Second World War. Digby was killed in action on 11 April 1945, aged twenty-three.

Francis Edward Beaufort (1887-1930)
Service number 41720
Private, 23rd Reinforcements

Arthur Dudley Cornes and Dorothy Bertha Cornes 1917

Arthur Cornes was a self-employed baker living in Grey Lynn, Auckland, when he enlisted on 14 November 1916. He and Dorothy had been married for only three-and-a-half months. Arthur was posted immediately to the 23rd Reinforcements for training and embarked with them from Wellington on 14 March 1917. The couple most likely visited the Berry studio for this double portrait when Dorothy came to Wellington for Arthur's farewell.

The army made good use of Arthur's civilian skills. After his arrival at Sling Camp in England on 21 May 1917, he was posted to the Army Service Corps to undergo a course of instruction in military baking. He joined the 1st New Zealand Field Bakery at Rouen, France, on 8 March 1918 and next day was formally appointed a baker. Arthur served with the Field Bakery until 14 December. He returned to Sling Camp, where he joined the 3rd Reserve Battalion of the Auckland Infantry Regiment.

Returning to New Zealand on 25 April 1919, Arthur was discharged from the NZEF on 23 May, classified as 'no longer fit for war service'. A medical board at Codford Camp in England had examined him on 30 January 1919 and reported that he was suffering from 'debility' after the 'stress and strain' of ten months continuous active service. Working in the Field Bakery had been no easy job: as the historian of the Army Service Corps recorded, 'Field bakers and cooks sometimes worked in knee-deep mud, at the same time trying to maintain adequate hygiene standards.' The raw conditions had taken their toll on Arthur's health: the Codford board reported that he had suffered from myalgia (muscle pain) and looked 'anaemic'. He felt occasional pain in his left shoulder and his lumbar region in cold weather, and his left shoulder 'creak[ed] a little'. Nonetheless, the board thought at that stage he had 'no definite arthritis', and assessed his 'degree of disablement' for pension purposes at 'less than 20%'.

After the war, Arthur returned to his trade as a baker, and despite his health issues was to live a long life. In the local body elections of 1941 and again in 1944, he was a succesful candidate for the Mt Eden Borough Council. In October 1968, as the fiftieth anniversary of the Armistice approached, Arthur applied to the Defence Department for the medals to which he was entitled: the British War Medal and the Victory Medal. Dorothy Cornes died in 1958, and Arthur in 1971.

Dorothy Bertha Cornes (1893–1958)

Arthur Dudley Cornes (1884–1971)
Service number 40518
Private, 23rd Reinforcements

Jack Langley Braddock 1917

Before Jack Braddock left to serve on the Western Front, he had this picture taken. He is holding a pace stick in his left hand and a New Zealand Army 'lemon-squeezer' hat in the other. Pace sticks were commonly used in the Army by instructors to ensure soldiers marched at a regular pace.

The son of Frederick and Edith Braddock of Lyall Bay, Jack attended Wellington South School. When he attested for general service in December 1916, he was living in the Wellington suburb of Melrose and working as an apprentice signwriter at Smith & Smith Ltd in Cuba Street. Jack's great grand-niece, Amy Braddock, recalls that Jack had an uncle who worked at the Berry studio and may possibly have taken this portrait. Jack was a promising artist, taking design classes at technical college in the evenings after work. Had he come from a wealthier background, he might have gone on to study the fine arts.

In the course of training in New Zealand, Jack was promoted to lance corporal in March 1917. Leaving New Zealand on 5 April, he disembarked at Devonport, England, two months later. On 6 July, after four weeks' training, he left for France and was posted to the 1st Battalion of the Rifle Brigade, and his unit fought at Passchendaele in early October.

One of the deadlier diseases that sporadically broke out among close-quartered troops was cerebrospinal meningitis, which had a particularly high mortality rate during those years before the advent of penicillin. Jack contracted the disease on 3 December, in the midst of a ferocious snowstorm, and died just two days later at a casualty clearing station. He was buried near Ypres in Lijssenthoek Military Cemetery, the second-largest Commonwealth cemetery in Belgium. His service is commemorated, along with that of twenty-two other former pupils and teachers, on the memorial gates of Kilbirnie School in Wellington.

Jack Langley Braddock (1895–1917)
Service number 44439
Rifleman, New Zealand Rifle Brigade

Cecil Theobald Coate 1917

Cecil Coate was born in Wellington on 15 December 1889. As a young man he was a keen cricket and soccer player for the Karori clubs, and worked as a clerk for the Wellington Harbour Board. He married Nora Maud Furness on 15 March 1916.

Cecil had volunteered for military service in 1915, but was rejected for having varicose veins. In December 1916, after conscription was introduced, his name was drawn in the second ballot, and he attested for service on the 28th. He was posted to train with the 25th Reinforcements on 8 January 1917 and on 2 February was transferred to the 24th Reinforcements.

Sailing from Wellington on 5 April, Cecil underwent further training at Sling Camp in England with the 4th Reserve Battalion, Auckland-Wellington Regiment in June and July, when he was sent to France. On 24 July he joined the 3rd Battalion, Wellington Infantry Regiment.

At Passchendaele in 1917, Cecil's battalion was part of the force that successfully drove the German defence from Gravenstafel Spur on a cold and rainy 4 October. During the attack, Cecil was hit in the face by an enemy bullet. He was admitted the same day to No. 3 New Zealand Field Ambulance, then to No. 3 Australian Casualty Clearing Station; on the following day, he was sent far behind the lines to hospital at Le Tréport, on the French coast. Though a medical report noted in March 1918 that the wound had caused him 'periodic attacks of frontal neuralgia' (excruciating nerve pain in his face), Cecil can be considered lucky. The success of the attack on Gravenstafel misled British commanders into thinking enemy resistance was weakening, but the terrible casualties that ensued later in the month – which included 845 dead New Zealanders – would prove them wrong.

On 23 December, Cecil was posted in a training role to the 3rd Reserve Battalion of the Wellington Infantry Regiment at Sling Camp and, except for one week's leave in September 1918, served with them until he embarked for New Zealand on 7 February 1919. On 23 April, he was discharged from the NZEF as 'no longer physically fit for war service on account of wounds received in action'.

Cecil spent the rest of his life in Wellington, where he continued to work for the Harbour Board. Nora passed away in 1949, and Cecil on 14 November 1950, aged sixty.

Cecil Theobald Coate (1889–1950)
Service number 44447
Private, 24th Reinforcements

Adolph Goldfinch and Ann Goldfinch, with James, Arthur, Eileen and Charles 1917

Adolph Goldfinch declared that he was forty-three years old when he attested for military service at Taumarunui on 5 January 1917. This was not true: he was, in fact, born on 21 October 1859, in Wellington. The doctor who performed the medical examination, and made a note of Adolph's grey hair, must have been a little sceptical.

Adolph's marital history also gives lie to his claims of youthfulness. He had married Mary Edith Robinson in 1878 and they had ten children. His second marriage (which appears not to have been officially registered) was to Mary Tremain Day, and they had five children, one of whom died in infancy. These are most likely the children in the portrait, but the woman is probably Ann Goldfinch, who was Adolph's wife at the time he departed overseas.

Prior to the war Adolph had been a self-employed labourer. He appears in newspaper reports several times, for his contracting business and also for bankruptcy in 1895. He is also on record for failing to send his children to school, and between 1906 and 1908 he was sentenced three times to one month's imprisonment with hard labour for disobeying maintenance orders. Maybe the war offered something of an escape, for which he was prepared to falsify his age.

After training with the 24th Reinforcements, Adolph embarked for England on 5 April 1917. He was first based at the Sling training camp in Wiltshire, then the nearby garrison town of Larkhill, returning to Sling in April 1918. By all accounts, he was a theatrical and engaging character. He wrote poetry and acted. In England, the army gave him a job as an entertainer in the training camp. He was, of course, much older than the average soldier, and in July he was found unfit for service. He finally returned to New Zealand on the *Ulimaroa* on 7 November 1918. Adolph died in Hamilton on 3 June 1927 from an embolism of the heart.

clockwise from top

Adolph Goldfinch (1859–1927)
Service number 45853
Private, 24th Reinforcements,
Wellington Infantry Regiment

James Goldfinch (1912–51)

Arthur Goldfinch (1913–unknown)

Eileen Goldfinch (1915–unknown)

Ann Goldfinch, née Moore (unknown)

Charles Goldfinch Day (unknown)

John Blair Crossan 1917

John Crossan was the son of Scotsman John Crossan and his English wife, Jane. The couple came to New Zealand around 1890, and young John was born in Normanby in 1894. He worked as a bricklayer before enlisting to join the New Zealand Field Artillery, 24th Reinforcements, in January 1917. His military uniform includes a bandolier over the left shoulder and riding spurs. He trained at Featherston Camp before embarking on the *Pakeha* for Plymouth, England, in April 1917.

John trained with the Field Artillery at Chadderton and Aldershot, and spent a month in the New Zealand hospital at Codford undergoing treatment for venereal disease. VD was a common infection among troops and was frowned upon by the military authorities, who regarded it as a self-inflicted wound. But sickness did not prevent John from being sent to France in February 1918, where he served as a cook for the Field Artillery's 7th Battery. He relinquished this appointment on 14 June, when he was evacuated to hospital. In August, he was posted to the New Zealand Entrenching Battalion. John eventually left England for New Zealand on 27 May 1919, and was discharged from the NZEF on 23 December 'on account of illness'.

John returned to New Zealand and to his previous occupation as a bricklayer. In 1923, he married Dorothy Lilian Griffin. In 1934, aged forty, he was arrested in Wellington and fined, along with a fellow bricklayer John Barwood Murray, for drunkenness and evading a tram fare.

John Crossan died, aged seventy-three, on 15 November 1966. He lies in the Returned Services Section of the Old Levin Cemetery.

John Blair Crossan (1894–1966)
Service number 42958
Gunner, 24th Reinforcements,
New Zealand Field Artillery

William John Adam Prussing 1917

William Prussing was thirty-six years old and working as an able seaman for T Ricketts of Port Nelson, when he attested as a volunteer for the 24th Reinforcements on 19 October 1916. His father, also William, was German by birth but had lived at Collingwood and Nelson for many years, and his mother, Ellen, was Scottish.

William's military record reveals little about his war service other than several periods of hospitalisation. Entering training camp on 4 January 1917, he embarked from Wellington for England on 26 April. He was posted to the Rifle Brigade's 5th Reserve Battalion at Brocton Camp, Staffordshire, on 21 July and on 7 December left to serve on the Western Front in France. He joined the 3rd Battalion, New Zealand Rifle Brigade on 31 December. He may have been wounded or sick in January, as he was reported as rejoining his unit from a field ambulance on 29 January 1918.

William was wounded on 29 March, when a bullet struck his face, leading to a round of hospital stays in England. He was sent first to No. 2 New Zealand General Hospital at Walton-on-Thames, Surrey, then to the convalescent hospital at Hornchurch, Essex, till 8 May, when he was granted two weeks' leave, with orders to report to Codford Hospital in Wiltshire.

He was back at Brocton Camp on 23 July, then returned to active service with his unit on 30 September. On 11 October, William was wounded again. This time a bullet fractured his left arm, and he was evacuated again to hospitals in London and Birmingham, then to Hornchurch in December as a convalescent.

William embarked from England for the voyage home on 1 March 1919 and was discharged from the NZEF on 7 November, 'no longer physically fit for war service on account of wounds received in action'.

William never married and lived with his brother-in-law in Hawke's Bay. He died at Hastings on 18 January 1965, aged eighty-six.

William John Adam Prussing (1880–1965)
Service number 42870
Rifleman, 24th Reinforcements,
New Zealand Rifle Brigade

William John Main and an unidentified woman 1917

William Main's daughter identified him as the soldier in this portrait. The woman is still unidentified; she looks too young to be his mother, Helen Main, who would have been sixty-one when the photograph was taken.

William was born in Helensville in 1895. When he attested for military service on 1 November 1916, he was single, living in Wellington and working for New Zealand Railways as a cadet. He named Helen, who lived in Remuera, Auckland, as his next of kin.

Entering training camp on 3 January 1917, William was posted to the Signals Section of the 25th Reinforcements' Specialist Company; his railways experience would have made him familiar with telegraph and telephone equipment.

He embarked from Wellington on 26 April and marched into Sling Camp in England on 20 July. He immediately joined the Canterbury Infantry Regiment's 4th Reserve Battalion, but was transferred to the Otago Infantry Regiment's 4th Reserve Battalion on 5 September. William qualified as a First Class Signaller on 22 November. He was sent to France on 11 January 1918, where he was transferred to the 1st Battalion of the Auckland Infantry Regiment on 17 February.

On 3 April, William was admitted to hospital suffering from 'PUO' (pyrexia of unknown origin), an acronym often used for various fevers; one of these was trench fever or 'five-day fever', a widespread infection transmitted by body lice. For the rest of the year, William was to spend considerable time in hospital and convalescent camps. On 23 June he was transferred to No. 1 Entrenching Battalion, then to the 2nd Battalion, Auckland Infantry Regiment on 27 August, but he was hospitalised again on 5 September. His record cites both dysentery and enteritis as likely infections – certainly, both were rife in the trenches. Invalided to Brockenhurst Hospital in England on 27 September, William was discharged on 5 November and sent to the New Zealand Convalescent Depot at Torquay. On 2 December, he embarked for New Zealand, where he was discharged from the NZEF on 6 February 1919.

William married Grace Victoria Cobb in 1922. He died at Wellington on 25 July 1947, aged fifty-two.

William John Main (1895–1947)
Service number 42762
Private, Signals Section of the
25th Reinforcements' Specialist Company

Richard Arthur Williamson 1917

Richard Williamson was born on 5 August 1896 at Taita in the Hutt Valley, where his parents, Alexander and Emma (née Parkinson), were farming. When he attested for military service on 7 December 1916, he was working as a farmer for F T Williamson at the small Waikato township of Gordonton.

Richard commenced training with the 25th Reinforcements on 6 February 1917, and in this portrait wears their collar badge, featuring a warrior with a taiaha. He was promoted on 14 March to lance corporal and to corporal on 23 April. Some time between these dates, probably not long before his embarkation from Wellington on 26 April, Richard visited the Berry studio to have his portrait taken.

Disembarking at Devonport, England, on 20 July, Richard marched into Sling Camp the same day. He was posted to the 4th Reserve Battalion of the Auckland Infantry Regiment with the rank of lance corporal and was sent on 5 September to France, where he remained at Étaples Camp for about a month. On 11 October, he went to the front, where he joined the 1st Battalion of the Auckland Infantry Regiment. He was still a lance corporal, but on 12 November he relinquished the rank at his own request and reverted to private.

A gunshot wound in the neck on 3 April 1918 saw Richard hospitalised in England until he was discharged to the New Zealand Command Depot on 9 August. On 3 October, he was back at Sling Camp with the Auckland Infantry Regiment's Reserve Battalion, and on 4 November he was ordered to attend a training course for non-commissioned officers at Tidworth, once more a lance corporal. He was back with his battalion at Sling by 10 December as a private, having again relinquished his rank.

Richard embarked at Tilbury for the voyage home on 12 April 1919 and arrived at Wellington on 30 May. He was discharged from the NZEF on 27 June.

Returning to the Waikato, Richard took on a dairy farm at Puketaha. During the Second World War, he served with the Home Guard as company sergeant major of the Waiuku Battalion, by which time he was married to Elizabeth Mary Riddell and had become a father of two.

Richard died at Rotorua Hospital on 9 January 1981, aged eighty-four.

Richard Arthur Williamson (1896–1981)
Service number 46155
Lance corporal, 25th Reinforcements

Harold John Batten 1917

John Batten, the son of Alfred and Lucy Batten, was twenty-four years old when he commenced service on 5 January 1917. At the time he lived in Otaki and was working as a horse trainer and jockey.

After training with the New Zealand Rifle Brigade, John embarked on the troopship *Pakeha* from Wellington on 26 April 1917 as part of the 24th Reinforcements. In England he rejoined the Rifle Brigade. Harold's unit endured the terrible fighting at Passchendaele in October 1917, where he was wounded in his left upper arm by an exploding shell on the 12th. This was the worst day of the entire war for New Zealand, when 845 men died and over 3000 were wounded. The high casualty figures stemmed in part from the failure of the Allies' creeping barrage during the attack on Bellevue Spur: this was an attempt by the artillery to give close-range cover to advancing infantry, but many of the shells fell short and hit the New Zealanders.

John was lucky to survive. He was hospitalised in England: first at Lewisham in London, then at Walton-on-Thames, Surrey. A compound fracture of the humerus was suspected, but an X-ray revealed no breaks. His detailed medical case sheet describes the surgeons' work on 4 December: first to search for foreign bodies, then to mend the tissue damage. 'It was found impossible to bring the severed muscles together', the report reads, adding that the skin edges were 'brought together with considerable tension – one small part being left uncovered as the edges would not meet'. An inspection of the arm a week later found the 'upper wound looking beautiful', but the skin over the lower wound was sloughing due to tension and required further surgery; the area was prepared for a skin graft, but there is no evidence John received such. In January, he needed a further operation to treat abscesses.

After returning to New Zealand on the *Maunganui* in February 1918, John was discharged from military service on 13 August, deemed 'no longer physically fit on account of wounds received in action'. Later that year, he married Bessie Olive Taylor in 1918; they had two children, Patricia and Ernest. John Batten lived in Hamilton until the age of sixty-one and died on 1 April 1955.

Harold John Batten (1892–1955)
Service number 44182
Rifleman, New Zealand Rifle Brigade

Harry Luckman and Ellen Isabella Luckman, with Harry George 1917

This portrait was probably taken shortly before rifleman Harry Luckman's embarkation with the 25th Reinforcements on 26 April 1917. He was a butcher by trade, and the 'griddle' badge on his sleeve may refer to his appointment as the troopship's butcher.

Harry was born in England on 3 September 1891. According to a family story, at the age of eighteen he joined the crew of a ship sailing to New Zealand, but 'jumped ship' in Wellington. He went to Tokomaru Bay, where he found a job in the freezing works. In 1915 he married Ellen Isabella Denham, and baby Harry followed soon after. By the time Harry's name was drawn in the first ballot for military service on 16 November 1916, they were living in Feilding, where he worked for the Feilding Bacon Company. He appealed against his call-up, stating that he had three brothers at the front and another two working in munitions factories, and that his family would suffer undue hardship if he was sent into camp. But the board dismissed his appeal and he left home for training on 5 February.

Entering Sling Camp in England on 10 July, Harry joined the Rifle Brigade's 5th Reserve Battalion. He embarked for France on 14 September, and on 8 October joined the Brigade's 1st Battalion, in readiness for the attack on Passchendaele four days later. Harry survived the first day's carnage, but late on the 13th he was buried by an exploding shell. His commanding officer reported that Harry was 'quite demented' when he was dug out; indeed, Harry had to be 'almost carried' to the regimental aid post, and he was later diagnosed with severe shell shock.

Hospital spells followed; one report noted that Harry had 'marked hesitancy of speech and increased reflex action', and that he complained of 'pains in legs' and could not remember the explosion. In January 1918, a medical board billed him unfit due to 'neurasthenia', and he boarded the troopship *Tahiti* for New Zealand on 1 February. Harry was discharged from the NZEF on 11 June.

According to his family, nightmares troubled Harry in the postwar years, and his marriage broke down. He died on 18 November 1977, aged eighty-four; Ellen had died in 1966. Their son, Harry George, served in the army during the Second World War. He died in 2001 and is buried near his father in the soldiers' section of Wellington's Makara Cemetery.

Ellen Isabella Luckman, née Denham (1893–1966)

Harry George Luckman (1916–2001)

Harry Luckman (1891–1977)
Service number 46051
Rifleman, 25th Reinforcements,
New Zealand Rifle Brigade

Elliott Hoffer 1917

At the time of his enlistment, Elliott Hoffer was a fitter for the Wellington Gas Company, and lived with his Russian-Jewish parents, Soloman and Ethel Hoffer, in Ghuznee Street. Though he was single at the time, he is listed as having two people dependent on him, presumably his parents, who (according to his attestation) were naturalised in Wellington. Elliott is the only Jewish soldier in the Berry collection.

Elliott had his first medical inspection on 1 September 1916, but was rejected as unfit for military service on account of 'bad feet and heart trouble'. As time went on, the NZEF could less afford to be as choosy. Elliott passed a second inspection on 3 January 1917, and was attested for service with the NZEF the same day. He was twenty-eight years old. On 20 January, the *Evening Post* reported that he had been sent to training camp the previous day with 31 other Wellington men 'towards making up the city's shortages in the 25th Reinforcements'.

Elliott embarked from Wellington aboard the transport ship *Willochra* on 9 June 1917 as part of the 26th Reinforcements. He most likely sat for his portrait in the lead-up to departure. He disembarked at Devonport, England, on 16 August, and went on to Brocton Military Training Camp in Staffordshire. On 23 October, he left Brocton for France, arriving at Étaples Camp on 26 October. After further training, he was sent to the front lines, where he joined the 2nd Battalion, New Zealand Rifle Brigade. Elliott remained on active service with his unit until 6 August 1918, when he was detached for training at the 3rd Army Musketry School. The musket was, by then, obsolete, but the term was retained to refer generally to small arms, such as the rifle and machine gun. He rejoined his battalion on 15 September, then on 16 October went on leave to the United Kingdom.

On 27 May 1919, Elliott left England aboard the transport ship *Tahiti*, bound for New Zealand, where he was discharged from the NZEF on 3 August. He married Elsie Beatrice Schultz the following year. They had a daughter, Ethel Betty Hoffer, in 1923, and the family moved to Palmerston North, where Elliott worked as a plumber.

Elliott died on 20 July 1958 in Palmerston North and is buried there at Kelvin Grove Cemetery.

Elliott Hoffer (1888–1958)
Service number 45378
Rifleman, New Zealand Rifle Brigade

Claude Carey Ballinger 1917

Born on 8 April 1894, Claude Ballinger was nearly twenty-three years old and working as a storeman at the Wellington warehouse of Ballinger Brothers, 'Manufacturers and Suppliers of Plumbers' Requisites', when he enlisted on 21 February 1917. His forebears had founded the company late in the previous century, but the family name is perhaps better known in sport shooting circles. The Ballinger Belt, presented annually by the National Rifle Association of New Zealand, is the country's oldest sports trophy.

Claude married Ivy Hilda Standen on 2 May 1917 (inset) and sailed from Wellington on 9 June with the 26th Reinforcements. He arrived at Sling Camp in England on 16 August and was posted for training to the 4th Reserve Battalion of the Auckland-Wellington Regiment.

Claude's initial medical examination recorded that at some point he had suffered from lead poisoning and from rheumatism in the left leg. What it did not disclose was a condition noted during a later exam: since the age of seven he had been 'troubled by giddiness and pains in [the] cardiac area' and that he had had to give up outdoor work. He was ordered out of a route march in October and sent to Codford Depot for nine weeks of 'light duty', followed after 30 November by 'graduated training'. A medical board on 15 February 1918 now recorded the facts about his weak heart, diagnosing 'DAH' (diffuse alveolar haemorrhage). It noted that he still appeared 'debilitated and anaemic' and had made 'no improvement' after the months at Codford. Yet another medical board, on 25 June, reported Claude's 'shortness of breath on exertion', and that his progress was 'stationary'. It assessed him as permanently unfit for military service, and fit only for 'light duties' in civilian life. It further recommended that he be discharged from the NZEF and not be considered eligible for a pension on the grounds that he had 'suppressed his illness before board & in camp in N.Z.'.

Returning to New Zealand, Claude was duly discharged on 16 July 1918. Despite his heart condition, however, he was to enjoy a long life, dying on 27 July 1969 at the age of seventy-five.

Claude Carey Ballinger (1894–1969)
Service number 50982
Private, 26th Reinforcements

Charles Henry Faulkner and Edith Faulkner, with Edwin and Eslet 1917

This family portrait of Charles and Edith Faulkner and their children would likely have been taken before Charles left for overseas service in 1917. Nine-year-old Edwin proudly wears a sailor suit, and baby Eslet is supported in the gentle grip of her parents.

Charles was born in Dunedin on 2 August 1879; when he enlisted in October 1916 he would have been thirty-seven years old. Although he was working at the time for Wilson & Canham, a wool and hide merchant in Thorndon, he lists his pre-war occupation as 'cook' – and it was primarily in this capacity that he would serve his country overseas, which entitled him to extra pay.

In January 1917, Charles was posted as a private with the 24th Reinforcements. Entering Sling Camp on 28 July, he was transferred to the 4th Reserve Battalion of the Canterbury Infantry Regiment. His record states that in November he underwent 'a course of instruction in cooking and [was] considered competent to superintend cooking of any regular unit'. Leaving for France on 13 December, he arrived at Étaples on the 16th, but three days later was hospitalised with sciatica. The army sent him back to England, to No. 2 New Zealand General Hospital at Walton-on-Thames, by which time his sciatica had become severe. By February 1918, though, he was clearly well enough to take on mild duties, and by June he was working in the hospital kitchens.

Walton was New Zealand's first military hospital in England, set up in August 1915 to care for the first intake from Gallipoli. As casualties mounted, the hospital was extended by adding annexes, including the hotel at Oatlands. Converted from a former stately home, Walton offered a pleasant environment. According to *The War Effort of New Zealand* (1923): 'The food and cooking received special attention, and it is only necessary to question any New Zealanders who were patients in the hospital to ascertain whether they were not well satisfied with the meals supplied to them!'

After the war's end, with repatriation still months away, Charles worked in the kitchens at Sling Camp, finally taking off his cook's cap in March 1919. On 10 May he sailed for New Zealand and was discharged on 21 July.

Charles Faulkner died in Marton on 27 September 1958. Edith died in Lower Hutt on 17 June 1959, and is buried in the Karori cemetery.

Edith Faulkner (1879–1959)

Edwin Faulkner (1908–1961)

Eslet Faulkner (1916–2003)

Charles Henry Faulkner (1879–1958)
Service number 41520
Private, 24th Reinforcements

James Gillham 1917

James Gillham attested for military service on 20 April 1917. He was twenty-three years old and had been an inmate of His Majesty's Reformatory, Invercargill, for two years.

Born in London on 18 March 1894, James arrived in Wellington in 1913, working as a ship's steward. He 'jumped ship', found a place to live and found work at the Wellington Club, with burglary as a sideline; during May–July 1914 he broke into and ransacked eight houses in the Aro Valley area. He was arrested on 11 August for these offences, and for the theft of £300 worth of jewellery at Whanganui on 6 August.

James pleaded guilty to the charges and on 30 September was sentenced to two years' hard labour on each charge, to run concurrently, plus three years' 'Reformative Detention'. After serving six months in Wellington Prison, he was sent to Invercargill. He was recommended for probation in April 1917, provided he be accepted for service in the NZEF. Released on 30 April, he trained with the 28th Reinforcements.

James embarked from Wellington on 14 July 1917, disembarked at Plymouth on 24 September and marched into Sling Camp the same day. He joined the 4th Reserve Battalion of the Otago Infantry Regiment there and was sent to France on 26 October. On 17 January 1918, he was accidentally injured when a lorry ran over one of his feet after he had slipped into a ditch. He rejoined his unit on 1 February, but was back in hospital on 16 February suffering from the effects of a gas attack.

Sent to England on 29 March, James was admitted to Mile End Military Hospital, then to the New Zealand Convalescent Hospital at Hornchurch on 9 April. On 7 June a medical board classified him as unfit for military service due to 'chronic pulmonary disease, indeterminate', attributed to the gassing. James returned to New Zealand on 8 October and was discharged from the NZEF on 19 December.

James went back to England in 1920, where he married in 1922. He and his wife Winifred set up home in Dagenham and had eight children. In later life James worked as a school caretaker; he was regarded as a pillar of his community and was an active member of his local Catholic parish. He died on 28 September 1974 and is buried with Winifred in St Patrick's Cemetery, Leytonstone.

James Gillham (1894–1974)
Service number 54131
Private, 28th Reinforcements

Arthur Chote 1917

Born in Wellington on 1 September 1886, Arthur Chote was working as a self-employed dairy farmer when he enlisted at Woodville on 21 March 1917.

He entered training camp on 12 April, joining the 28th Reinforcements. Later than month, he was transferred to the 27th and embarked with them from Wellington on 16 July. Arthur disembarked at Liverpool on 16 September and marched into Sling Camp the same day. He trained with the Canterbury Infantry Regiment's 4th Reserve Battalion but was hospitalised at Tidworth from 14 to 22 November, when he returned to Sling. Sent to Étaples in France on 5 December, he commenced active service a month later with the 1st Battalion, Canterbury Infantry Regiment. Arthur was still with his unit on 28 August – a remarkable achievement given the intense fighting in which the battalion was involved during those months.

Arthur went on leave to the United Kingdom on 6 November 1918 and was back with his unit on 26 November. He had a spell of occupation duty with the battalion in Germany, and more leave in Britain in February 1919. He embarked for the return voyage to New Zealand on 10 May 1919 and was discharged on 21 July.

After the war, Arthur returned to farming, in the Dannevirke area. He never married, and in November 1938, after some years of failing health, he was found dead on his farm at Kiritaki 'in circumstances pointing to heart trouble'. He was buried in the nearby cemetery at Mangatera.

Arthur Chote (1886–1938)
Service number 52952
Private, 27th Reinforcements

Alfred Featherston Gower 1917

Alfred was one of three Gower brothers, all farmers, who served in the army during the war. As well as sitting for his solo portrait, Alfred also posed for a double portrait (inset) with his older brother Gerald (see page 106), who – at 6 feet 4 (1.93 metres) – is clearly the taller of the two.

When New Zealand entered the war, Alfred, aged twenty-three and farming at Omoana in Taranaki, was quick to volunteer. He enlisted as a trooper in the Wellington Mounted Rifles on 18 August, and on 15 October embarked with the Main Body for training in Egypt. But his time there was to be short. On 17 April 1915, he was hospitalised with a strained groin; it was severe enough to send him back to New Zealand, and on 17 August he was discharged from the army as 'medically unfit for active service'.

Alfred returned to his farm, but volunteered again for service in 1917, this time with Gerald. Alfred entered Trentham Camp on 30 May as a private in the 28th Reinforcements. During their training, the brothers' grandmother died in Palmerston North. They attended the funeral but were late returning to camp, and were punished with the loss of one day's pay for this – and, in Alfred's case, for being found in a hotel bar while on active service. However, this escapade did not prevent Alfred's promotion to lance corporal on 25 July.

Arriving at Sling Camp in Wiltshire, England, on 24 September, Alfred was sent on to the Rifle Brigade's camp at Brocton, Staffordshire, on 3 October, where he joined the Brigade's 6th Reserve Battalion. Twenty days later, he was sent to the front, where he joined the New Zealand Rifle Brigade's 1st Battalion.

Alfred's service record notes that on 19 June 1918 he was injured when a grenade exploded 'under his nose' and that he 'was not to blame' for the accident. After treatment at a field ambulance he rejoined his unit on 6 July. But when wounded again on 24 August, with a gunshot wound to his left hand, he was evacuated to England and hospitalised at Walton-on-Thames.

Alfred's war was over. He embarked for New Zealand on 8 January 1919, where he was discharged from the NZEF on 21 March. Having returned to farming, he married Mabel Maud Mason in 1920. Alfred died in New Plymouth in 1976.

Alfred Featherston Gower (1891–1976)
Service number 11/479
Rifleman, New Zealand Rifle Brigade

Gerald Gower 1917

Gerald Gower was twenty-seven years old and living at Petone when he voluntarily attested on 1 March 1917. He trained with the 28th Reinforcements at the same time as his brother Alfred (see page 104) and, like him, was charged with being late returning to camp from their grandmother's funeral.

Embarking from Wellington for overseas service on 26 July, Gerald marched into Sling Camp in England on 24 September and on 3 October was sent north to the Rifle Brigade's training camp at Brocton. In early November he was admitted to the 3rd New Zealand Hospital at Codford to be treated for venereal disease. He stayed there for a month, but was back at Codford on 31 December, suffering this time from measles. He returned to Brocton on 11 February 1918, where he qualified as a marksman on 6 March.

Gerald was sent to France on 20 March and joined the New Zealand Rifle Brigade's 2nd Battalion. He was involved in heavy fighting as the Germans advanced during their spring offensive. When this advance failed, the Allies began to drive the German forces back. In August 1918 Gerald's unit was engaged in the Second Battle of Bapaume, one of the decisive turning points of the war. On the 26th he received a gunshot wound to his right thigh, and he was evacuated to hospital. After discharge from hospital, Gerald did not return to the fighting, but was posted to No. 2 New Zealand (Area) Employment Company. Employment companies put non-combatant men into a range of temporary roles, such as traffic control, salvage and construction work and guard duty.

Embarking for New Zealand on 3 March 1919, Gerald was discharged from the NZEF on 15 December and graded 'no longer physically fit for war service' due to arthritis.

Gerald returned to farming, initially at Kohuratahi, inland from Stratford, and later near Te Awamutu. He married Emma Doris Lee in 1923 and died in Hamilton on 25 February 1972.

Gerald Gower (1890–1972)
Service number 55949
Rifleman, New Zealand Rifle Brigade

James Alexander Matheson and Ethel Louisa Gertrude Matheson 1917

James Matheson served in the New Zealand Dental Corps. His promotion to regimental sergeant major took effect from 1 April, so the photograph was probably taken shortly afterwards, given the brand-new appearance of his uniform (still lacking Dental Corps collar badges).

James stands somewhat protectively behind his wife, Ethel. The couple had married on 24 February 1917 and it is possible that by the time of the sitting they already knew she was expecting; their daughter, Monica Ethel, would be born on 2 December.

James was born in Dunedin on 11 July 1881. Before the war, he worked as a theatrical agent, promoting films for the Kinemacolor Company of Melbourne. 'Kinemacolor' was an early colour motion-picture process.

James volunteered for military service in early December 1915. Due to a problem with his left foot, he was graded as 'fit for home service'. He joined the Dental Corps at Trentham the next day, as an orderly with the rank of private, but was promoted corporal on 6 February 1916 and to sergeant major on 17 April.

New Zealand had made an early commitment to caring for troops' teeth. Two dental officers went out with the Samoa force in August 1914, and the New Zealand Dental Corps proper was formed in 1915. In the war's early stages, civilian dentists worked at the training camps to equip recruits with a healthy mouth. This was no small feat: in *The War Effort of New Zealand* (1923) Thomas Hunter reports that the 1998 men of the 17th Reinforcements required '6335 fillings, 5237 extractions, and 854 dentures', with '371 fillings, 48 extractions and 32 dentures still remained to be done on board the transports'. The Dental Corps also worked overseas, coping with heaving decks at sea, sandstorms in Egypt, and shelling in France; among those they treated were British and French troops, who were invariably astonished and delighted to find there was no fee attached. There were also New Zealand dentists based at hospitals in England, and another, yet more grim task of the Dental Corps lay in identifying the dead from dental records.

As an orderly, James Matheson probably did not work directly on teeth. He served with the Dental Corps until demobilised on 6 February 1919. He died in Auckland on 23 June 1942.

Ethel Louisa Gertrude Matheson, née Williams (1889–unknown)

James Alexander Matheson (1881–1942)
Service number 3/2266
Regimental sergeant major, New Zealand Dental Corps

Harry Spire Powell 1917

Harry Powell was thirty-six years old and farming at Reikorangi, near Waikanae, when he enlisted. Born in Wiltshire, England, he had emigrated to New Zealand with his parents at the age of three. He was their only son.

He embarked from Wellington on 13 August 1917 on the troopship *Mokoia* with the 29th Reinforcements, New Zealand Field Artillery. Only four days into the voyage, however, Harry was admitted to the ship's hospital with an injury to his left knee. He had been on parade on deck when he slipped and twisted the knee inwards. He spent three days in hospital and was left with an injury that meant he was unable to walk without pain. On 10 May 1918, Harry went before a medical board at the Field Artillery's base at Ewshot Camp, near Fleet in Hampshire, England. The board noted that he was still suffering pain in his knee and was unfit for marching or guard duty. He was declared permanently unfit for active service, but classified as 'C2' – fit for home service. He was sent to the NZEF Discharge Depot at Torquay on 2 September and back to New Zealand, where he was discharged from military service on 6 March 1919.

On 11 September 1919, at Wellington, Harry married Myrtle Irene McLaughlin. He died in Levin on 12 February 1955, aged seventy-four.

Harry Spire Powell (1881–1955)
Service number 50519
Lance bombardier, 29th Reinforcements,
New Zealand Field Artillery

Harold Pilkington and an unidentified woman 1917

Harold Pilkington was born in Bolton, Lancashire, on 22 July 1897 and came to New Zealand with his widower father, James, in 1910. He had just turned twenty and was working as a labourer for the Gear Meat Company at Petone when he volunteered for service with the 34th Reinforcements on 23 July 1917. He commenced his training at Trentham Camp two days later, and embarked for overseas service on 13 October with the 30th Reinforcements. Harold was promoted to lance corporal on 10 October, so this photograph must have been taken some time prior to that date. The young woman with Harold is unidentified.

Harold disembarked at Liverpool on 8 December 1917 and entered Sling Camp the next day. As was routine with new arrivals at Sling, he lost his New Zealand promotion and reverted to the rank of private for his advanced training. He left England for France on 15 April 1918, and two days later joined the 2nd Battalion of the Wellington Infantry Regiment for active service.

Gas poisoning and burns to the neck saw Harold hospitalised and homeward bound. On 20 May he was admitted to No. 1 New Zealand Field Ambulance; he was transferred the next day to a casualty clearing station, thence on the 22nd to hospital at Rouen. He was sent to England on 25 May, where he was admitted the next day to No. 1 New Zealand General Hospital at Brockenhurst. From there it was on to Codford on 10 June, where he convalesced.

As with other New Zealand troops overseas, however, repatriation took time. Harold finally left England on 21 November 1919 and arrived in New Zealand on 13 January 1920. He was discharged from the NZEF on 2 February.

Harold married Naomi Lankshear in 1923. He continued working for the Gear Meat Company as a manager, living in Lower Hutt until his death in 1979.

Harold Pilkington (1897–1979)
Service number 61767
Private, 30th Reinforcements,
Wellington Infantry Regiment

Robert Managh and Margaret Young Managh 1917

Robert and Margaret Managh had been married just four months when this picture was taken. Robert's uniform shows collar badges of the 29th Reinforcements, and he was later to serve overseas with the New Zealand Machine Gun Corps.

Robert was born in November 1889 at the small village of Sixmilecross in County Tyrone, Northern Ireland, and emigrated to New Zealand in 1913. He and Margaret were married on 31 March 1917, and in May, at the age of twenty-one, Robert attested for army service. At the time, he was working in Marton as a ploughman.

Robert entered Trentham Camp on 28 June, in the 30th Reinforcements. On 25 July he was transferred to the 29th Reinforcements and remained with the unit for a month. It was during this period that the couple sat for their portrait at the Berry studio. At the time, newspapers were giving casualty figures from the bloody fighting at Messines. Luckily for Robert, he would return safely from only brief service at the front.

Posted to the 30th Reinforcements, Robert embarked on 13 October 1917 for England, where his first posting was to the Auckland Infantry Regiment. In April he was hospitalised at Codford for a bout of 'pleurodynia', or Bornholm disease, a viral infection of the chest. Though intensely painful and often frightening (another name for the disease is 'devil's grip'), pleurodynia is usually over within a week or so. Robert was posted in June to the New Zealand Machine Gun Corps, and it was with this unit that he marched into camp at Camiers, France, on 3 October 1918. Following the Armistice in November, Robert returned to New Zealand in 1919 and was discharged on 22 July.

Robert and Margaret farmed near Marton, and later retired to Whanganui. Robert died in 1966; Margaret had passed away eleven years earlier, in 1955.

Robert Managh (1889–1966)
Service number 59401
Private, 29th Reinforcements

Margaret Young Managh, née Glen (1888–1955)

Ernest Walter Reeve 1917

This rather damaged studio portrait shows Ernest Reeve, who was born in Martinborough in July 1892 to parents William and Mary.

Prior to enlistment, Ernest was working as an engine driver in Wellington at the New Zealand Government Railway Workshops. In his attestation on 6 August 1917, Ernest stated that he had served in Sydney with the 7th Australian Light Horse in 1915 and the New Zealand 16th Reinforcements in 1916, and that he was also a current member of the Territorials. He had contracted lumbago while on duty and had an old back injury caused by falling from a horse, which put him out of action for eighteen months, but the recruiting officer clearly saw promise in Ernest, noting, 'This man is most willing and I think the training would improve him.'

Unfortunately, these words proved overly optimistic. Ernest embarked with the 32nd Reinforcements from Wellington aboard the *Tahiti* on 16 November 1917, destined for Liverpool. But his injury flared up again, and he was sent back to New Zealand, embarking from Plymouth aboard the *Ionic* on 24 August 1918. He was treated for neuritis (inflamed and painful nerves) at King George V Hospital in Rotorua the following year. Because his injury pre-dated his war service, and he had not actively served, he was not recommended for a soldier pension.

The few details we know about Ernest's later years reflect those of many men who found their lives permanently unseated by the war and its effects. He married and tried to run a small dairy in Auckland. However, he mistreated his wife and was known to drink, and they divorced in 1930. Ernest Reeve died in Auckland on 28 May 1948.

Ernest Walter Reeve (1892–1948)
Service number 63934
Private, 32nd Reinforcements

Frederick David Mason Smith 1917

Frederick Smith was born in Wellington on 25 February 1896 and grew up in the suburb of Karori. His grandfather William Smith, born 5 May 1843, would have been one of the first Pākehā born in Wellington. Fred, as he was known, was almost twenty-one at the time he attested for service on 8 February 1917. He already had some military experience, as he was employed by the Defence Department as a member of the Garrison Artillery and had previously served with the 5th Regiment in Wellington. After enlisting, he trained as a gunner with the Field Artillery.

Posted to the 32nd Reinforcements, Fred embarked for England on 21 November, exactly two months after sitting for this portrait. He marched into the Field Artillery's training depot at Ewshot in England on 8 January 1918 and was sent to France on 28 March. There, Fred was posted to No. 3 New Zealand Entrenching Battalion on 19 May, and served with them for nearly a month. On 15 June he was posted back to the Field Artillery. He received a gunshot wound to his left hand on 8 October and after treatment in France was sent to England. Fred eventually sailed from Southampton for the return voyage home on 4 October 1919, disembarking at Auckland on 15 November. He was discharged from the NZEF a month later.

Fred married Constance Priscilla Luxton in 1926. During the early 1940s he served as a secretary of the Returned Services Association's Hutt Valley branch. He died in 1971.

Fred's uncle was Major William James Hardham, New Zealand's sole recipient of the Victoria Cross during the South African (Second Boer) War, and the first New Zealand-born man to receive the medal. William served also in the First World War; wounded at Gallipoli, he returned to become a well-known figure in Wellington, playing an active role in the RSA and at Anzac parades until his death in 1928.

Frederick David Mason Smith (1896–1971)
Service number 50898
Gunner, New Zealand Field Artillery

Walter George Scambary and Ida Emily Scambary, with George Eric 1917

Walter Scambary was born in Barraba, New South Wales, and came to New Zealand with his mother and siblings around the turn of the century (his father, James, was by then deceased). He had two sisters, Rose and Maud, and five brothers – Norman, Tom, John, Francis (Frank) and Arthur (see page 122) – all of whom joined up to serve New Zealand. Walter's name was drawn in the fourth ballot in February 1917. At the time, he was living in Kilbirnie, Wellington, and working as a salesman; he was also a member of the New Zealand Garrison Artillery.

Walter embarked from Wellington on 21 November 1917 on the troopship *Maunganui*, bound for Liverpool, as part of the 32nd Reinforcements, New Zealand Field Artillery. Stationed initially at Ewshot Camp in Hampshire, Walter went over to France in February 1918, where he served with the Field Artillery. He specialised in the use of the 9.45-inch heavy trench mortar. Nicknamed the 'Flying Pig', this was a massively built version of the trench mortar, which was essentially a tube that fired a bomb at a steep upward trajectory so that it fell directly down on the enemy, making it ideally suited for the trench warfare in which Walter was engaged.

Walter eventually returned to New Zealand on the *Tahiti* in May 1919. He went home to Ida and George in Kilbirnie, sustaining his interest in weaponry as an active and highly acclaimed member of the Aotea and Petone rifle clubs. He died on 12 September 1968, aged seventy-six.

Walter's brother Norman, a driver in the Field Artillery, fought in the Gallipoli campaign and died in France in January 1918, aged twenty-two; he is named on the Kilbirnie School War Memorial. Tom, an engine driver from Okahukura, was posted to the 45th Specialist Company but does not appear to have gone overseas. John, a cook by trade, served on the Western Front with the Machine Gun Corps during 1917, but was sent home the following year, thanks to chronic inflammation of the left knee. Frank was also with the Machine Gun Corps in France from late 1916. Though he was frequently laid low with a painful ear infection, he saw out the war overseas, returning to New Zealand in April 1919. Sadly, Frank committed suicide by drowning on 16 November 1925.

Ida Emily Scambary (1895–1990)

George Eric Scambary (1916–1990)

Walter George Scambary (1892–1968)
Service number 50897
Gunner, 32nd Reinforcements,
New Zealand Field Artillery

Arthur James Scambary and Mary Scambary 1917

Arthur and Mary (known as Molly) Scambury were married on 4 November 1916. Born 18 May 1890, Arthur was originally from New South Wales, and came to New Zealand in 1903 or 1904. Like his five Australian-born brothers, he was to serve with the New Zealand forces (see also Walter Scambary, page 120). He lived in the Wellington suburb of Kilbrnie, working as a carpenter for L Driscoll, a builder and decorator in Seatoun.

Arthur first volunteered for service in January 1916, but was turned down because he suffered from chronic sycosis, a skin condition. Vision in his right eye was variable, too, as a result of a blow to the face five years earlier.

After applying again – successfully – in April 1917, Arthur was posted the 28th Reinforcements, and later transferred to the 32nd Reinforcements, New Zealand Field Artillery. But he was never to serve overseas. At a medical examination at Featherston Military Hospital in October that year, he was diagnosed with ear trouble, apparently resulting from a pre-existing case of scarlet fever. The examiners found him 'unfit for service' for an 'indefinite' period, and recommended he be discharged.

Arthur returned to civilian life, and on 7 August 1918, he and Molly had a son. Arthur died on 31 December 1958, aged sixty-nine, and was buried at Karori.

Mary Scambary, née Mahonie (1891–1965)

Arthur James Scambary (1890–1958)
Service number 56035
Gunner, 32nd Reinforcements,
New Zealand Field Artillery

Creighton Chesnutt 1917

Creighton Chesnutt was born in Kilcar in Donegal, Ireland, on 20 January 1890 and came out to New Zealand as a single man in 1914 to join the New Zealand Police Force. Prior to his enlistment in 1917, he was a constable based at the Mt Cook Barracks, Buckle Street, Wellington. Creighton's bright orange hair was noted in his military file.

On 12 April 1917, Creighton entered camp to join the 28th Reinforcements, but on 28 April he was transferred to the 27th Reinforcements; it was as a member of this unit that he was photographed at the Berry studio, as shown by his collar badges. He was further transferred to the 33rd Reinforcements and promoted to corporal on 19 June, embarking from Wellington with them on 31 December.

At Sling Camp in England, Creighton reverted to the rank of lance corporal and was attached to the 'Composite Reserve Battalion' of the 4th New Zealand Infantry Brigade, prior to being sent to France to join the 1st Battalion of the Otago Infantry Regiment on 16 September 1918.

At the end of the war, Creighton returned to New Zealand and, following demobilisation, rejoined the police in Wellington. In 1921, he married Nellie Messenger. The couple moved to Taranaki and then to Taihape, where Creighton continued to serve with the police from 1938 to 1955.

Creighton was an impressive 101 years old and one of New Zealand's last surviving First World War veterans when he died at Tauranga on 2 June 1991, by which time he had ten grandchildren.

Creighton Chesnutt (1890–1991)
Service number 53473
Private, 27th Reinforcements

Louis Wager 1917–18

Louis Wager was born in Heybridge, Essex, in 1888, to Martha and Frederick Wager. The Wagers came out to New Zealand shortly before the First World War.

Louis was rejected at his first attestation for military service, owing to chest trouble and flat feet. He attested again, successfully this time, in March 1917, expressing a preference for a posting to the Artillery. He was twenty-eight years old at the time and working as a 'grocer's traveller' for Sibun Ltd, a grocery store in Petone. He probably made home deliveries, a service much in demand in an era when few families possessed a car. He listed his mother as his next of kin, giving her address as 278 Cuba Street.

His prior medical state, coupled with contracting influenza and pneumonia in 1918, seems to have further hindered Louis' ability to serve, and he was discharged in 1919 after a further medical report, which dismissed him with a tersely worded 'poor physique'. But he did well to survive the 1918 influenza pandemic: it was particularly lethal in the damp, crowded military camps at Trentham and Featherston.

In 1949, Louis married Jane Elizabeth Wickenden. For most of his life he worked as a travelling salesman for Sibun. He died in 1965 in Wellington at the age of seventy-six and is buried in Karori Cemetery.

Louis Wager (1888–1965)
Service number 77744
Private, NZEF

Herbert James Freeman and Marguerita Freeman, with Zena 1917–18

Herbert Freeman, his wife, Marguerita, and baby Zena lived in Featherston, where Herbert worked as a house painter before his war service.

Herbert attested for service on 18 December 1916, but was granted leave for four months on the grounds of 'hardship', having appealed on the grounds that his wife was 'a very delicate woman'; she was probably pregnant at the time with Zena. They later had a second war baby: Rita Haydon Freeman, born 22 April 1918.

After training at Trentham between March 1917 and 31 July 1918, Herbert was assigned to the New Zealand Rifle Brigade, 42nd Reinforcements, embarking for London on the *Tofua* on 1 August 1918. He was based at Sling Camp in Wiltshire for a short time at the end of the war, then returned to New Zealand on the *Briton* in June 1919.

After the war, the family lived in the Masterton area until 1928. Herbert and Marguerita had two more children, Leslie and Jack. They moved to Sydney, but were back in New Zealand by 1930, and Herbert and Marguerita lived in Hamilton for the rest of their lives. Herbert died on 7 May 1950, and Marguerita died in 1975.

Marguerita Freeman (1885–1975)

Zena Freeman (1917–2013)

Herbert James Freeman (1889–1950)
Service number 48013
42nd Reinforcements
New Zealand Rifle Brigade

Unidentified families 1916–18

The Berry collection of soldier portraits features fourteen family portraits; six families remain unidentified. Whereas many soldiers would have walked into the Berry studio off the street to have their photograph taken, family groups would have made an appointment. This is very much evidenced by the care that the family members have made in their dress. The Brown family (lower left) obviously visited Berry & Co. in the midst of a chilly Wellington winter, the bitterness of which perhaps permeated the studio walls that day. The women, perhaps the soldier's sisters, are lavishly dressed, their winter coats enriched with furs. The portrait sitting was obviously viewed as an 'occasion'. Along with a string of pearls and corsage of miniature daffodils, the seated woman wears the NZEF insignia as a brooch just above her top button. Adapted military badges could be readily purchased from local jewellers for soldiers to present to family members and sweethearts. Worn publicly, such insignia declared that the wearer had a loved one at war.

The older women in the Banks photograph (top left) also wears an NZEF brooch. She might be Mrs SL Banks of Whanganui, the mother and next of kin of Leonard Rye Banks (service number 23/1936), an upholsterer who embarked from Wellington 4 March 1916 with the 4th Reinforcements, New Zealand Rifle Brigade. Of five soldiers named Banks who served in the Rifle Brigade during the First World War, Leonard is the most likely to be the man in this family portrait. He was wounded in France in September, but survived the war and lived until 1973.

The cheerful little girl in the Henderson group (top right) proudly wears the insignia of the New Zealand Army Medical Corps – The Rod of Asclepius, a serpent-entwined rod – in support of her father. Asclepius was a Greek deity associated with healing and medicine.

Unidentified soldiers and family members, with inscriptions
clockwise from top left

'Banks' 1916–17

'Graham' 1918

'Henderson' 1917–18

'Simpson' 1917

'Chiss', or 'Hiss', or 'McNiss' about 1918

'Brown' 1917–18

Eric Edward Marchant 1918

Eric Marchant was born to Henry and Henrietta Marchant in Wellington on 30 January 1898 and was later enrolled at the Te Aro School. He had just turned twenty when he enlisted for the NZEF on 1 February 1918; by then, he had been part of the New Zealand Garrison Artillery in Wellington for eight months. Eric was 5 feet 3 inches (1.6 metres) tall and weighed only 97 pounds (44 kilograms); the medical examiners found him undersize and underweight and therefore unfit for active service, but they judged him fit to serve with the troops occupying Samoa, which Germany had peacefully surrendered in 1914. He completed his service there and was discharged on 13 March 1919.

Eric moved to Australia after the war. He had a relationship with a woman listed on the electoral roles as 'Charlotte Marchant', but there is no record of their marriage. In 1940, he married Margaret Doreen Ledran in Sydney, but the pair did not have any children. Eric mainly worked in hotels as a steward or porter. Eric died in Nottingham, England, on 29 March 1957, aged fifty-nine.

Eric Edward Marchant (1898–1957)

William James Leonard Bowker 1918

Born 1901 in Sydney of an Australian father and Scots mother, William Bowker was three months shy of seventeen when he enlisted on 8 February 1918. At the time, he was working at the New Zealand Clothing Co. in Cuba Street, a stone's throw from the Berry studio, where he posed for this portrait in his hat and great coat.

Classified at his medical inspection as 'probably fit', William was appointed to Home Service in the New Zealand Army Ordnance Corps. The New Zealand Army Ordnance Corps was founded on 1 February 1917. Its function was to support the fighting troops by managing the Army's stores of ammunition, uniforms and equipment. William remained on New Zealand soil for twenty months as a clerk and store worker on the Corps' permanent staff. William discharged himself from the NZAOC on 24 June 1919 and lived in Auckland for a while, before he rejoined the permanent force. From 28 November he served as a gunner in the Royal New Zealand Artillery. Early the following year he appears to have been part of the small expeditionary force detached to Fiji to help the British colonial authorities quell a sugarcane workers' strike. A doctor's note, written at Suva in March 1920, records that William suffered sore feet 'resulting from septic mosquito bites aggravated by playing football'.

William quit the Artillery on 10 May 1920 and, just one week later, enlisted as a private in the Medical Corps. In 1926, he married Florence Iris Lindegreen.

In May 1940, William returned to the Artillery, but again he would remain on home turf. This would have been a plus for the family, since he was now a father of two. He listed his most recent employment as an insurance superintendent for the New Brighton Borough Council. Posted to the 18th Heavy Battery, William was stationed at Battery Point, on the northern shore of Lyttelton Harbour, where his unit manned a pair of 4-inch naval guns. Lyttelton had been defended by gun emplacements since the 'Russian scare' of the late nineteenth century; now, in the wake of Pearl Harbor, it was considered vulnerable to attack from Axis powers. Infamously, in the early hours of 25 June 1941, a German minelayer entered the waters off Godley Head and laid ten mines, then slipped away.

William was discharged from the Artillery in September 1941, and from military service altogether in September 1948. He died in 1976.

William James Leonard Bowker (1901–1976)
Service number 148
Cadet, New Zealand Army Ordnance Corps

William Alexander Larkin 1918

William Larkin was the eldest of the five children born to John and Annie Larkin. At eighteen years old, he attested for service on 18 February 1918. He had been working as a machinist with Hutcheson, Wilson and Co., a Wellington firm better known today as Hutchwilco. The army must have valued his skills, for when he was posted to the New Zealand Army Ordnance Corps, it was as an artificer – an engineer trained in making specialist equipment, such as weaponry.

William faces the camera squarely; he was no doubt proud to be following in the footsteps of his father, John, and his uncle, Frederick William, both of whom served overseas and fought on Gallipoli. Although they both returned to New Zealand, the influenza pandemic claimed not only John's life on 21 November 1918, but also that of Frederick the following day.

In September 1920, William was transferred to the Ordnance Stores in Wellington, and he appears to have worked here until his discharge, at his own request, on 24 January 1921. His discharge papers state that he was of 'very good' character, and give his work qualifications as 'sailmaster' – presumably another skill he had picked at Hutcheson, Wilson and Co.

In 1924, William married Evelyn Thelma Pycroft, from Karori. She was three years his junior. They settled in Featherston and the Hutt Valley and had eight children. William worked on a farm for most of his life. He died in 1951, aged fifty-two. Evelyn died four years later.

William Alexander Larkin (1899-1951)
Service number 163
Private, New Zealand Army Ordnance Corps

Edwin Mitchell 1918

Edwin Mitchell sat for his portrait in his New Zealand Army Ordnance Corps uniform, with the ribbon of the Queen Victoria Jubilee Medal on his tunic. Edwin was listed in a 1917 Wellington street directory as a labourer. The following year he was listed as a 'Defence Department employee', living at 7 Garrett Street, just around the corner from Berry & Co.'s studio in Cuba Street and a short walk away from the Ordnance Depot in Buckle Street.

Edwin was born in London in 1853 and had served with the Royal Marine Light Infantry. He attested for service with the New Zealand Army Corps on 2 April 1918 and remained a member until his discharge on 14 February 1921.

Members of the Ordnance Corps based in New Zealand were often older men with useful trade skills such as blacksmithing, harness-making and carpentry. A man of Edwin's age with military experience could also make a useful contribution to support the war effort, and Edwin served as a nightwatchman. Edwin died in 1938, aged 85.

Edwin Mitchell (1853–1938)
Service number 79
New Zealand Army Ordinance Corps

Thomas Christopher Gollins and Grace Caroline Gollins, with Graham Thomas 1918

Thomas Gollins was born in Ashburton on 13 May 1890. Before he came to live in Wellington, in about 1914, he was living on the West Coast. He was a keen cyclist and in September 1912 became a local hero for winning the 'Round the Mountain' bicycle race in Taranaki. He also had strong political opinions, and associated with some of the local founders of the Labour Party. In August 1911, he attended a 'mass meeting' at Runanga, a mining town with a reputation as a centre of radical politics, which was called to campaign actively against compulsory military training. The meeting voted to form an 'Anti-Conscription League' and Thomas was appointed to the committee, which was to work towards the aim of establishing branches of the league all over New Zealand. Before his enlistment Thomas was working in Wellington as a motor mechanic and chauffeur. He married Grace Twist at St Paul's Pro-cathedral, Wellington, on 13 July 1915.

Surprisingly, given his political background, Thomas's enlistment on 25 August 1916 was voluntary. He was passed as fit, but was not attested for service until 27 January 1917. He entered training camp on 12 April 1917, when he was posted to the 28th Reinforcements, later transferring to the 29th Specialist Company, Machine Gun Section, a move which may have been influenced by his background as a motor mechanic.

Thomas and Grace's son Graham was born on 13 February 1918. The trio visited the Berry studio for farewell photographs, shortly before Thomas embarked for the war on 23 April.

In June, Thomas spent a week in hospital at Suez suffering from diarrhoea, then in July he was hospitalised at Faenza, Italy, with influenza. He marched into Sling Camp in England on 29 July and was posted to the Reserves of the Canterbury Infantry Regiment. In October he was sent to the machine-gun training centre at Belton Park, Grantham. After the Armistice, he remained in England for 1919, during which he served as a driver. Finally embarking on 15 January 1920, he arrived home in New Zealand on 6 March, almost two years after he left, and was discharged from the NZEF on 28 April.

Thomas returned to his work as a mechanic and, later, as a garage proprietor in Wellington, Levin and Hawera, where he died in 1944. Grace died in Rotorua in 1982. Graham Gollins served in the Royal New Zealand Air Force in the Second World War and died in 1988.

Thomas Christopher Gollins (1890–1944)
Service number 53492
Private, New Zealand Machine Gun Corps

Graham Thomas Gollins (1918–1988)

Grace Caroline Rebecca Gollins, née Twist (1893–1982)

Alfred Hart and Queenie Hart 1918

Despite the plain appearance of their clothing, this portrait of Alfred and Queenie Hart was taken on their wedding day, 19 April 1918. The couple had met at their workplace, printer-publisher Whitcombe and Tombs, in late 1916: Alf had worked there as a type compositor since he was fifteen, and Queenie, originally of Masterton, was a letterpress machinist. Perhaps Queenie wore everyday garb because the couple had to fast-track their wedding plans: Alf was to disembark with the 38th Reinforcements, New Zealand Field Artillery on 24 April, having completed five months' training as a gunner.

Alf was Emma Hart's third son to enlist. His older brothers, Harry – who had already served in Samoa – and Jack, had embarked for Europe in early 1917. Perhaps thankfully for Emma, who was a widow, her son Bill had failed the military medical exam and remained in Wellington with the Territorials. Alf trained with the Field Artillery at Aldershot, and went to France in September 1918, where he was a driver of the horses that pulled the heavy artillery carriages. Once the war was over, he returned to Wellington – and the arms of his mother and wife – on 26 August 1919. He resumed his old job, and he and Queenie welcomed the first of their four children, a boy, on 24 June 1921. The couple lived happily together into their eighties.

Alf's brother Jack was wounded in action in October 1917 and again in September 1918 at the Somme. His wounds were severe enough to see him sent home on the *Marama* in December 1918 and hospitalised for several months at Trentham. Later, in 1921, he married and moved to Auckland.

Their brother Harry did not fare so well. Harry, who had suffered shell shock, gas poisoning and burns in the field, returned to New Zealand in December 1919. While he initially returned to his job as a printer, he was admitted to Trentham Military Hospital in July 1920 for 'neurasthenia', a condition that today is known as post-traumatic stress disorder. The following month, he attempted suicide and was transferred to Porirua Hospital, in a condition described as 'one of melancholia with suicidal tendencies'. Having seemingly improved, Harry returned to Trentham Military Hospital in March the following year, but was tragically found dead on 17 June 1921, having taken his own life. 'Delusional insanity and exhaustion' was cited as the cause.

Hilda Queenie Hart, née Dixon (1897–1981)

Alfred Hart (1896–1978)
Service number 65391
38th Reinforcements

George Mackay Scott 1918

George Scott was born in Wellington on 28 December 1895. His father, also George, was a Scotsman from Fife, and his mother, Thirza, was English. Theirs was a large family: George had four brothers and four sisters. He enlisted on 5 May 1915, aged nineteen, giving his address care of his mother at 24 Constable Street, Wellington. He was employed as a hardware assistant at the firm of Duthie & Co., established by John Duthie, who was appointed mayor of Wellington in 1889 and helped found the *Dominion* newspaper. On George's right sleeve are three inverted chevrons, signifying that he has served overseas for three years, so this photo would have been taken to mark his return to Wellington.

George had embarked from Wellington on 9 October 1915 with the 2nd Battalion of the New Zealand Rifle Brigade, serving in Egypt and France in 1916 and 1917. On 18 June 1916, he was admitted to a casualty clearing station near the front line, and from 24 July 1917 to the New Zealand Convalescent Depot at Torquay, England. On 1 February 1918, he embarked for New Zealand, classified as 'permanently unfit', and was discharged from the NZEF on 15 April as 'no longer fit for war service', because of goitre.

George married Emma Kate Gapper in 1920, and they had a daughter, Norine, born in Eltham in October of that year. He enlisted again in 1940, the early stages of the Second World War, and on his military record Emma is given as his next of kin. At the time, they were living in Karori, and he worked as a sales manager at the Vacuum Oil Company.

George Scott died at Levin in 1976, and Emma outlived him by eight years.

George Mackay Scott (1895–1976)
Service number 24/273
Rifleman, New Zealand Rifle Brigade

Francis Barber 1918

On 6 December 1916, Wellington's *Evening Post* newspaper published the names of soldiers who had recently been awarded the Military Medal. The MM, established on 25 March 1916, was awarded to non-commissioned soldiers for bravery on the battlefield, and one of those receiving the new decoration was Private Frank Barber of the New Zealand Army Medical Corps.

Frank had sailed from Wellington as a member of the Field Ambulance section of the Main Body on 16 October 1914. Front-line service in the Medical Corps was one of the most dangerous jobs in the army. Like the fighting troops, medical personnel had to cope with brutal conditions at the front. Amid shells, small-arms fire, poison gas, barbed wire, mud and rain, they would stretcher wounded men to a regimental aid post for a quick check and patch-up; from there, they took casualties to a Field Ambulance dressing station to be triaged and accordingly treated or sent further behind the lines to hospital. The pace was often intense: during the Battle of the Somme, one dressing station treated an average of 110 casualties per hour.

Stretcher-bearers in particular won the admiration of fighting troops, especially when they went out into no man's land to rescue wounded soldiers and bring them in for treatment. Frank won his medal for his gallantry during the battle of Chunuk Bair on Gallipoli on 7–8 August 1915, for bringing wounded men in under heavy enemy fire. We know from Frank's medal citation that after his service on Gallipoli, he served on the Western Front in 1916.

Frank returned to Wellington on 12 May 1917 on a ship carrying 517 other sick and wounded soldiers, but his homecoming was not a happy one. In his absence his wife had had an affair with another man and a child had been born to them. Divorce proceedings began; at a court hearing in June 1918, Frank petitioned successfully for the marriage to be dissolved on grounds of his wife's misconduct, and the other man was ordered to pay him £25 damages.

We know when Frank – medal sported proudly on his chest, and sergeant's stripes on his arm – visited the Berry studio because 'April 18' is inscribed on the negative. At that time, the court hearing was impending, but in September, he was to marry again, to Dorothy Eveline Chant. He and Dorothy lived in Island Bay, Wellington, and later in Inglewood, Taranaki. Frank died on 10 May 1968, aged seventy-seven, and Evelyn on 3 February 1984. They are buried together in the Services section of Te Henui cemetery, New Plymouth.

Francis Barber (1891–1968)
Service number 3/160
Sergeant, New Zealand Army Medical Corps

Kenneth Randall Mason 1918

Kenneth Mason, born 11 October 1897, worked as a clerk for the Commercial Union Assurance Company in Wellington prior to enlisting on his twentieth birthday. He listed his father, GT Mason of Goring Street, Wellington, as his next of kin, and left for England with the 39th Reinforcements on 13 June 1918

With prior experience as a senior cadet in Wellington's Divisional Signal Company, Kenneth was assigned as a sapper in the Divisional Signallers. Signallers played a crucial role in communications during the First World War; they were required to lay lines and to be proficient in several forms of visual communication, including flag, lamp and heliograph, as well as Morse code. Signallers were often placed near the front line, in vulnerable positions.

Kenneth, however, returned to New Zealand unharmed. He posed for a second portrait in the Berry studio, most likely some time after his return in August 1919. In this (inset), he poses in elegant civilian clothes, a handsome, eligible young city man. Kenneth died in Wellington in 1977, aged seventy-eight.

Kenneth Randall Mason (1897–1977)
Service number 71343
Sapper, 39th Reinforcements Divisional Signallers

Leslie John Hawker 1918

In this portrait, Leslie Hawker wears the uniform of a private in the New Zealand Army with a 'lemon-squeezer' hat. Although no rank or specific unit insignia are visible, the negative is inscribed with the name 'Hawker' and the month 'June', and the Berry studio's register number tells us that the photograph was taken after 1917. A final clue to Leslie's identity was the insignia on his epaulettes – not usually visible in the portraits – which confirms him as a member of the 40th Reinforcements.

Leslie was nineteen years and two months old when he enlisted on 18 February 1918. He was single, working as a hardware assistant for C & A Odlin Ltd., and living with his mother at 6 College Street in central Wellington. Leslie's medical inspection describes a young man, 5 feet 10 inches (1.78 metres) tall, with brown hair, hazel eyes and a fresh complexion. Leslie entered training camp on 1 May 1918 and embarked from Wellington on 10 July, the month after he visited the Berry studio.

On 11 September, Leslie marched into Larkhill Camp in England. He joined the New Zealand Infantry Brigade's 4th Reserve Battalion and trained with them until 3 October, when he was posted as a rifleman to the Rifle Brigade's camp at Brocton.

The Armistice meant that Leslie did not take part in combat operations, and he left England on 5 August 1919 on the return voyage to New Zealand.

Leslie married Shelagh Isabel Coghlan in Wellington on 17 January 1923; according to a news report of their wedding, the newlyweds settled in Nelson. Leslie joined the army again in the Second World War and served in New Zealand. He died in Auckland on 10 December 1982.

Leslie John Hawker (1898–1982)
Service number 79146
Private, 40th Reinforcements

James Arthur Hoverd and Florence Lilian Hoverd 1918

This portrait of James Hoverd and his bride Lilian was taken on their wedding day, 20 July 1918.

James was born on 2 October 1895 in Wellington, son of William and Elizabeth (née Clark). There were seven Hoverd children: Elsie, Ernest, William, James, Doris, Ruby and Violet (Ernest and Ruby died in infancy). James – or 'Jim' – was especially fond of Doris – 'Doll' – and would accompany her piano playing on his violin. Jim's father, William senior, won local prizes for his homegrown flowers and vegetables, and Jim inherited his father's green fingers: he would often slip out at night to collect horse manure from the road for compost.

Jim was the only Hoverd son to sign up. He had first enlisted in 1916, but because he had mild tachycardia (a fast heart rate), as well as slightly flat feet with corns, he was classified 'C1' – 'likely to become fit for service overseas after special training'. The C1 training camp, based initially at Featherston, later Tauherenikau, helped recruits build up their health, and many of them later joined the reinforcements. Jim was conscripted in 1917; by the time he entered Trentham in May 1918 as part of C1 draft, he was working as a storeman for Cocks & Co., the jewellers on Victoria Street, Wellington. (He had also worked briefly on the city trams.) After training, he was transferred to the 42nd Reinforcements, and later the 43rd.

Jim was granted leave without pay from 18 July and married Florence Lilian Davies two days later in Vogeltown, and the couple took time out of their wedding day to pose at Berry & Co. Lilian (as she was known) was the eldest daughter of Ernest and Sarah Davies, who had emigrated from England around 1905.

Returning from leave on 23 August, Jim underwent another medical exam. Because of ongoing problems with his heart and feet, he was classified unfit for overseas duty, but 'fit for service of some nature in New Zealand', and on 30 August he was issued with a certificate of leave. His military service was over.

After the war, Jim and Lilian moved to Nelson, where he worked as a nurseryman. They had two children, Dulcie (born 1919) and Norma (1923). By the mid-1930s the family was back in Wellington; Jim took a number of jobs as a storeman or warehouseman, breeding canaries in his spare time. Jim died at Hutt Hospital in 1966, aged seventy; Lilian lived a further eleven years.

Florence Lilian Hoverd, née Davies (1889–1977)

James Arthur Hoverd (1895–1966)
Service number 77670
Private, 43rd Reinforcements

William Anderson and Marion Anderson 1918

Born in Glasgow, Scotland, on 18 December 1897, William Anderson was twenty years old when he attested for service in January 1918. At this time he lived in Westport and was a purser for the Union Steam Ship Company. His parents, John and Marion Anderson, lived in Yale Road, Wellington. Her anxious expression and protective arm around William help us identify the woman in this portrait as his mother, Marion. William also had a brother, George, and a sister, Janet.

Although William attested for military service on 25 January 1918, he was granted four months' unpaid leave and did not enter training camp until 22 May. He had stated on his attestation form that he would have preferred to join the Artillery, but the army posted him to the 41st Reinforcements to train as a rifleman.

He embarked from Wellington on 1 August 1918 and marched into the Rifle Brigade's training camp at Brocton in the north of England on 4 October. Battle-hardened men, veterans of the Somme and Messines, were stationed there to train new recruits such as William, who trained with the Brigade's 3rd Reserve Battalion.

Staffordshire's raw climate was perhaps too much for William. On 28 October he was admitted to Cannock Chase Military Hospital suffering from influenza. William died three days later, the cause of death being recorded as pneumonia. He was buried at the nearby Cannock Chase War Cemetery, and for many years after his death William's 'sorrowing parents' and siblings placed memorial notices in the newspaper on the anniversary of his death. Marion died in 1953, aged seventy-six.

Marion Anderson (1877–1953)

William Anderson (1897–1918)
Service number 80719
Rifleman, 42nd Reinforcements

William John Wanden 1918

William Wanden was born 8 July 1898, in Blenheim. His parents later moved to the Wellington suburb of Wadestown. On 7th June 1918, just prior to his twentieth birthday, William voluntarily enlisted for military service. At the time he was working as a clerk in the Post and Telegraph (P & T) Department and also doing military training with the P & T Engineers.

William entered training camp on 31 July 1918, part of the C1 Draft. He was assessed as fit and on 23 August 1918 was promoted to lance corporal. On the 19 September 1918, William was transferred to the 47th Reinforcements for training prior to overseas service but following the signing of the Armistice he was granted leave without pay on 22 November 1918 and demobilised back to civilian life.

William married Lily Marguerita Williams in 1922 and died in 1985.

Three of William's Blenheim cousins served in the First World War, and two of them, Eric Wanden and Herbert Winn Wanden, were killed in 1918.

William John Wanden (1898–1985)
Service number 87482
Lance corporal, 47th Reinforcements

Alick Blyth and Maud Allison Blyth 1918

We believe that this is a portrait of Alick Blyth and his wife Maud, whom he had married in Sydney in February 1915. The only identifying badge Alick wears on his uniform is that of the New Zealand Expeditionary Force, which was a standard badge used by the 34th Reinforcements onwards. The Blyths ordered three postcards and twelve cabinet-size prints of this image.

Alick was born in Temuka on 31 October 1891 to Thomas and Mary Blyth, both of whom hailed originally from Scotland. When Alick, who was 6 feet (1.83 metres) tall and weighed 167 pounds (76 kilograms), enlisted in April 1918 he was twenty-six years old, working as a labourer at Staveley, Canterbury. Following training at Trentham, he embarked for England on 2 October 1918 with the 43rd Reinforcements. On 11 November, while they were still at sea, the Armistice was signed. Alick marched into Sling Camp and remained there until July 1919, when he was shipped back to New Zealand and discharged.

Alick and Maud returned to Australia after the war. Alick died in Sydney on 8 June 1965, and Maud predeceased him in 1956.

Alick Blyth (1891–1965)
Service number 78550
Private, 43rd Reinforcements

Maud Allison Blyth, née McKay (1885–1956)

Charles McLaren Turnbull
and Evelyn Hilda Turnbull 1918

At the time he enlisted for military service, Charles Turnbull was working as company secretary for Turnbull, Hickson & Gooder Ltd., a Wellington firm of printers and stationers. The fashionably dressed young woman is his wife, Evelyn. After enlisting for military service on 19 October 1917, Charles had married Evelyn in Wellington on 28 November; a notice in the *Evening Post* reveals that he was the only son of Mr and Mrs J Turnbull of Oriental Parade, and that she was the third daughter of Mr and Mrs J Tipling of Marion Street.

On his attestation form, Charles had expressed a preference to serve with the Medical Corps. He entered camp on 3 April 1918 and after one week's training with the 40th Reinforcements was transferred to Awapuni Camp near Palmerston North for specialised training with the Medical Corps. On 4 May he was assigned to the hospital ship *Marama* to serve as a medical orderly. He made two voyages on the *Marama* to the war zone, the first departing from Wellington on 1 June and returning on 21 September. His second embarkation was on 19 October, returning to New Zealand on 27 January 1919, following which he was discharged from the NZEF at Wellington on 18 February.

Charles and Evelyn continued to live in their Oriental Bay home in the postwar years. They were both well-known players with the Roseneath Tennis Club, and in the 1920s Charles was also active in the Roseneath and Oriental Bay Electors' Association, which was agitating for better road access to those prosperous but hilly suburbs.

Charles and Evelyn both died at the age of seventy-one in Wellington in 1960, Evelyn on 18 September and Charles on 3 December.

Evelyn Hilda Turnbull, née Tipling (1889–1960)

Charles McLaren Turnbull (1889–1960)
Service number 75655
Private, New Zealand Army Medical Corps

Arthur Gamon and Amy Gamon, with Kathleen 1918

Born in Cheshire, England, in 1880, Arthur Gamon emigrated to New Zealand in 1912 with his brother Harold, and both of them would enlist with the NZEF.

Having worked as a grocer's assistant in England, Arthur continued in the same occupation in Wellington. He married Amy Carr on 2 December 1914 and their daughter Kathleen was born on 20 June 1916.

Arthur attested for military service on 10 May 1918 and joined the 45th Reinforcements in training camp on 15 August. On his attestation form he had stated his preference to serve with the 'Ambulance', and on the 28th he was transferred to the Medical Corps for training at Awapuni Camp near Palmerston North. On 12 September he was sent to Wellington, assigned to the staff of the deputy assistant director of Medical Services. On 19 February 1919 he was transferred again, to serve with the Medical Corps at Featherston Camp until 2 March, when he was granted unpaid leave pending his demobilisation.

Arthur went back to his civilian life as a grocer, and died in Wellington on 19 January 1963, leaving behind daughters Kathleen and Nora. Amy had died on 24 December 1935, aged fifty-three. Kathleen, who had married Arthur Hargreaves in 1939, lived until 13 June 2003.

Arthur's brother Harold, who enlisted in 1915 and served with the Otago Infantry Batallion, was on overseas service for nearly four years. Shot in the right knee on Gallipoli, he spent a period of recovery on the Greek island of Lemnos and was later transferred to the Western Front. He would be discharged from the NZEF on his return home in January 1919.

Arthur Gamon (1880–1963)
Service number 86241
Private, New Zealand Army Medical Corps

Kathleen Gamon (1916–2003)

Amy Gamon, née Carr (1882–1935)

George Robert Burch 1918

George Burch was a master plumber by trade, born in Wellington in 1880 to English-born parents. He married Elizabeth Maude Norris on 11 April 1903.

Poor teeth delayed George's military service. He attested first in June 1915, but was rejected on account of the condition of his teeth, which was deemed 'not sufficient' and requiring a lower plate. A second attestation in January 1918 was successful; George entered camp on 23 May. He commenced active service two months later, by which time he had been transferred from the 41st to the 42nd Reinforcements. On 31 July, he was promoted to temporary lance corporal. He embarked for England aboard the *Tofua* on 2 August and on 4 October marched into Brocton Camp, Staffordshire. Returned to the rank of rifleman, he was posted into the brigade's reserve unit.

After the Armistice on 11 November, George, like many other New Zealanders, would have to wait for repatriation. Soliders who had been overseas longer were given priority for the return to New Zealand; George eventually returned on 20 August 1919.

In 1925, George and Elizabeth divorced. Later that year he remarried; his new bride was Alice Rose Dow. George died in Masterton on 15 May 1970.

George's nephew Robert, known as Bob, founded the well-known Wellington bookstore Arty Bee's Books.

George Robert Burch (1880–1970)
Service number 80736
Private, 41st Reinforcements

Richard Weir Battersby and Gladys Francis Maude Battersby 1917–18

Richard Battersby, with corporal's chevrons on his sleeves, posed for this portrait with his wife, Gladys.

Married to Gladys since 1915, Richard was twenty-four years old when he attested for service. The couple lived on Pitt Street, Wadestown, and he was employed as a clerk by New Zealand Railways. His name was drawn in the fourth ballot for compulsory military service on 13 February 1917, and he enlisted on 20 July. After a month's deferral due to a bad cold, he entered the training camp at Trentham in late August and joined the 31st Reinforcements. On 26 September, Richard was transferred to the 37th Reinforcements and promoted to probationary corporal. He reverted to the rank of private at his own request on 15 March 1918 but was promoted again to temporary corporal on 13 May.

Richard left Wellington with the 43rd Reinforcements on the *Matatua*, disembarking in England on 5 December 1918 – three weeks after the Armistice. He arrived too late for active service, but as he was a recent arrival, his repatriation was slow, and it was not until September 1919 that he left for New Zealand on the troopship *Ionic*, disembarking at Wellington on 25 October.

Richard and Gladys spent most of their long lives in Wadestown, with many immediate family living nearby. Richard was a member of the Wadestown Chess Club and the Wadestown & Highland Park Mens' Club. The family was also involved in the Wadestown Horticultural Society (formerly the Wadestown Cottage Garden and Beautifying Society). Both passed away in 1980, when Richard was eighty-six years old and Gladys eighty-eight.

Richard Weir Battersby (1893–1980)
Service number 63539
Corporal, 43rd Reinforcements

Gladys Francis Maude Battersby, née Williamson
(1892–1980)

Eric Richard Davies Graham 1918

Eric Graham volunteered to enlist on his twentieth birthday – 4 July 1918 – the age young men were allowed to enlist without parental permission. At the time, he was living with his mother, Emma Mary Graham, of Melrose, Wellington, and was working as a clerk for the Defence Department. Eric was Wellington-born, but both parents were Australian: his father was from Brisbane, and his mother from Adelaide.

At the time he attested for overseas service, Eric was already serving as a territorial (part-time) member of the New Zealand Garrison Artillery Volunteers (GAV). Eric would have received training through the GAV, and at his attestation he expressed a wish to join the Artillery.

Eric was posted as a private to the 45th Reinforcements on 14 August 1918, and entered Trentham Camp the following day. Four days later he was transferred to the 49th Reinforcements, New Zealand Field Artillery, and at some point he relocated to Featherston Camp. In this portrait, Eric wears the 'flaming shell' collar badges of the Artillery. He was promoted to temporary bombardier on 5 November, just days before the war's end. Demobilised from Featherston Camp on 29 November, he was discharged on 7 August 1919. Eric died on 17 May 1980, aged eighty-one.

Eric Richard Davies Graham (1898–1980)
Service number 86321
Gunner, Royal New Zealand Artillery

Thomas Shaw Hamilton and Muriel May Hamilton 1918

Thomas Hamilton was born in Dunedin on 4 October 1880 to Scottish parents, later moving to Gisborne, where he found work as a labourer. On 31 October 1912, Thomas married Muriel Grant, and the couple subsequently had two children – Edna Jean, born 1915, and Charles Thomas, born 1918.

Old enough to serve in the South African (Second Boer) War, he enlisted as a private in the 10th Contingent and set off from Poverty Bay in April 1902, just weeks before the war's end. Following his return, he was awarded service medals – the Queen's South Africa War Medal and the King's South Africa War Medal – and he is wearing their ribbons in this photograph.

In 1918, Thomas, now thirty-seven years old and working as a slaughterman and fencer in Gisborne, donned a uniform once more. He entered Featherston Camp in August 1918 and joined the 48th Reinforcements as a lance corporal. He did not, however, see any action. He was demobilised during his training in December 1918 following the Armistice.

In 1930, Muriel divorced Thomas on the grounds of desertion. Thomas died in Gisborne on 27 November 1953.

Muriel May Hamilton, née Grant (1892–1977)

Thomas Shaw Hamilton (1880–1953)
Service number 8698
Lance corporal, 48th Reinforcements

Frederick Lars John Beu 1918

Frederick Beu was born in Wellington on 13 March 1884. His father, John (Johann), was German and had come to New Zealand with his Swedish wife, Mathilda, some time prior to Frederick's birth. It seems likely that John came from Stralsund, a town on the Baltic coast of Prussia, which had strong trading links with Sweden, as the Beus gave the name Stralsund Villa to their home at 515 Adelaide Road, Wellington.

Frederick was one of four brothers who served with the New Zealand Army during the First World War; although the oldest, he was the last to enlist. His brothers Otto and Gustav fought with the Rifle Brigade, and Reinhold with the Auckland Infantry Regiment and the Machine Gun Company. They all survived the war.

Frederick was thirty-three years old when he was balloted for military service in early November 1917. He was working as an engineer for Blundell Brothers, proprietors and printers of the *Evening Post* newspaper, and was living at Stralsund Villa with his wife, Barbara (née Cooke), whom he had married in Christchurch on 3 June 1914. He entered training camp on 2 May 1918 and was posted initially to the 40th Reinforcements. During May and July he was transferred twice between the 44th and 45th Reinforcements at Trentham, confirmed in rank as temporary corporal on 16 May, and sent to Featherston Camp on 31 July. On 2 August he was transferred yet again to the C1 camp at Tauherenikau. This was the camp for men who had been medically graded as likely to become fit for active service after special training, and Frederick was promoted to the rank of company quartermaster sergeant on 19 September. On 1 November he was transferred to the 50th Reinforcements, and on 26 November, after the Armistice, he was placed on unpaid leave awaiting his demobilisation, which took place on 27 March 1919.

Frederick and Barbara were to have two children, Bernard and Barbara. Frederick died at Wellington on 29 June 1953, aged sixty-nine.

Frederick Lars John Beu (1884–1953)
Service number 79008
Company quartermaster sergeant,
40th Reinforcements

James Hall Boyd and Mary Louisa Boyd, with James Robert 1918

The Boyds ordered a 12-by-10-inch (30-by-25-centimetre) print of this family photograph, which depicts James Boyd, his wife Mary and their son, James Robert. James was born in Glasgow, Scotland on 23 April 1886, and immigrated to New Zealand around 1912. He married Mary, eldest daughter of Mr and Mrs TO Stokes of Wellington, on 8 January 1913, and she gave birth to their only child on 9 January 1914. In this photograph, four-year-old Robert wears a fashionable sailor suit.

A devout churchman, James was working as a 'home missionary' for the Presbyterian Church in Napier. When he was called up for service in 1918, the Presbyterian Church initially lodged an appeal on his behalf with the Military Board. But the *Evening Post* reported on 21 June that the Reverend Dr James Gibb withdrew the appeal, stating that '[i]t was the policy of the Presbyterian Church to let every man go who could be possibly spared', and as the church at which James officiated was within a reasonable distance of Napier, the reverend felt that 'arrangements could be made to carry on the work there'.

On 12 September 1918, James entered camp and spent time at both Trentham in Wellington and at Awapuni in Palmerston North, where he trained for the Medical Corps – such work would have suited James well, given his background. While James attended camp, Mary and Robert went to live with her parents in Taranaki Street, Wellington.

James did not see active service. Following his four months of training, he was demobilised on 10 January 1919. Tragically, Mary died in childbirth on 6 October in Wellington, aged just thirty-two – 'a woman pure and sweet', announced the death notice in the newspaper.

James remarried in 1922, and the church later gave him a parish in Taranaki. He retired in 1951, and died in 1967. His second wife, Edna, died fifteen years later.

James Hall Boyd (1886–1967)
Service number 89364
Private, New Zealand Army Medical Corps

James Robert Boyd (1914–1999)

Mary Louisa Boyd, née Stokes (1887–1919)

William Edward Melton 1918

William 'Ted' Melton's pose in this portrait displays the machine-gun proficiency badge on his arm; this, along with the collar insignia, identifies him as a member of the New Zealand Machine Gun Corps.

Machine guns were one of the most devastating infantry weapons of the war, as each gun could fire about 700 rounds per minute, more than fifty expert riflemen could in the same time. The New Zealand Machine Gun Corps had been founded in 1916, after the British Army decided to emulate Germany's methods and organise self-contained mobile machine-gun units to provide concentrated firepower when and where it was needed. A particularly effective tactic of machine-gunners was to train their weapons on an enemy position by day, and then fire on it after nightfall to cause maximum confusion.

Ted was born in 1897 to John and Mary Melton of Waimate, Canterbury, the second of five children. When balloted in 1917, Ted was twenty years old, living at Glenhope and working as a cleaner for New Zealand Railways; he became part of the Nelson quota for the 41st Reinforcements. The quota left Nelson on 30 April 1918; a newspaper report in August lists Ted among those in the 45th Reinforcements' Specialist Company, Machine Gun Section, who were 'classified as first-class machine-gunners and . . . entitled to wear the proficiency badge'.

With the war so nearly over, Ted is unlikely to have served overseas. Sporadic news reports in the 1920s indicate that he worked as a fireman aboard the Union Steam Ship Company ship *Mararoa*, one of the steamers of the Wellington–Lyttelton service. It seems, too, that he had a liking for drink and a hot head: he was fined for various drunken escapades in public, and in October 1923 he was imprisoned for a month following a fracas with a fellow seaman.

Ted served again in the Second World War as a sapper, but died of sickness in Egypt in 1941; his age at death is given as forty-one, which suggests he gave a false date of birth when re-enlisting. He is buried at Heliopolis War Cemetery, Egypt.

William Edward Melton (1897–1941)
Service number unknown
New Zealand Machine Gun Corps

Charles Caleb Vandersluys 1918

Charles Vandersluys visited the Berry studio twice: first in 1916 as a private (inset) and later in 1918 as a regimental sergeant major. Charles often travelled under the surname of Berrold as he disliked being referred to as a 'Dutchman'.

In 1893, Charles married Florence Letitia Ayres in Dublin. On their return to England he joined the Gordon Highlanders, a British Army infantry regiment drawn mainly from Scotland. After serving during the South African (Second Boer) War, he was discharged in September 1902, joining the regiment's reserve in January 1903. Four years later, he completed his service, but remained living in London, working as a driver.

Travel was clearly in the blood, because Charles and Florence seldom stayed put for long. They spent three years in Buenos Aires, then in August 1914 departed for Australia, embarking on the *Ruahine*. Their four children remained in England.

After six months in Australia, the couple moved on to New Zealand, where Charles enlisted with the NZEF. He served in the Military Police for 288 days, subsequently joining the Army Service Corps. By now over-age and afflicted by rheumatic fever, Charles was unfit for active service. He served instead at Trentham Camp, rising from the rank of private to corporal in September 1916 and sergeant in February 1917. In April, however, he returned to the Military Police and to the rank of private.

A case was brought against Charles Vandersluys in August 1918 by two recently discharged privates, Fisher and Boosey. Exactly what happened is not clear; there had been a fracas with Fisher, and both sides issued statements that may have involved false information. No action was taken against Charles; but he was discharged from the Military Police on 9 December 1918 and given leave without pay.

More drama was to follow. On 24 December, Charles and Letitia embarked for San Francisco on the *Aryan*, a cargo ship, working their passage as cook and stewardess, respectively. But there was a fire on board and the crew abandoned ship; Charles and his wife were among the survivors who reached the Chatham Islands by boat and were then transported back to New Zealand on the *Hinemoa*.

Little more is known of the couple, other than that they travelled to Sydney in January 1933, returning the following year.

Charles Caleb Vandersluys (1871–unknown)
Service number 33008
Regimental sergeant major,
New Zealand Military Police

John McVean Walker 1919

John Walker was an engine-driver, born in Dunedin in 1881. He was living with his family at 440 Adelaide Road in Newtown, Wellington when he enlisted at Trentham Camp on 13 February 1919.

John's military file records that he medically graded 'C2', 'fit for Home Service', and that he was promoted to sergeant the same day. As an engine-driver, John would have been qualified to operate the stationary steam engines that powered machinery in the workshops at Trentham Camp.

However his service with the Corps was to be brief as on 31 July he was discharged at his own request 'owing to not being able to secure suitable accommodation for his family'. John died in Wellington on 24 January 1964.

John McVean Walker (1881–1964)
Service number 431
Sergeant, New Zealand Army Ordnance Corps

Berry & Co.'s copy portraits

The Berry collection includes portraits of thirty soldiers who did not personally visit the Cuba Street premises. In fact, some of these sitters are obviously posing at competing studios, including Zak's, run by Joseph Zachariah in nearby Manners Street. It was common practice for photographers to re-photograph existing prints. Sometimes, during the war, photographs taken overseas were sent home and copied for family and friends, particularly if a soldier's departure had been too rushed for a new portrait sitting.

After the death of a serviceman, copies might be made of an earlier portrait to become memorials. Brothers John (top left) and Donald Jessen (top centre) from Mauriceville, Wairarapa, both died overseas. John, who was quite possibly the first volunteer in the Wellington region, was killed in action in France on 24 August 1918, aged twenty-eight, and Donald died of pneumonia in London on 23 February 1919. Their parents and sisters placed memorial notices in the *Evening Post*, and may also have ordered copy portraits of the men to use as memorial objects.

Often, copies were made from group portraits. William Vetori, (top right) for example, who embarked in November 1917, was obviously photographed as part of a group, but the person who paid for a copy – likely his wife, Armanella – asked Berry & Co. to crop out the other men in the photo. Armanella herself posed with her baby son, William Samuel Alfred Vetori, who was born while William was still away. She probably sent their portrait (bottom right) to William overseas, and he would have sent his portrait in return.

Some of the copy negatives depict soldiers who never visited New Zealand but who had relatives here. For example, James Bury, a sergeant in the British Army who died on 13 April 1918 in Belgium. His sister Alice Blundell Howell and his brother Robert Blundell Bury, however, emigrated to New Zealand in 1910 and 1926; a framed Berry print, presumably ordered by Alice, was kept in the Howell homestead.

Not all copy prints originated from portraits taken in studios, of course – or even indoors, as testified by the unusual plein-air photograph of Albert Bailey (lower left), taken in 1915, probably at Featherston or Trentham training camp. Albert was working as a solicitor's clerk in Napier when he enlisted in 1915. He fought at the Somme and in November 1916 earned special mention for gallantry from the British commander, Field Marshal Haig. But the interwar years brought hardship for Albert. In financial straits after losing his house in Napier in the 1931 earthquake, he committed fraud and stole more than £2000, which earned him five years in prison.

clockwise from top left

John Jessen (1890–1918)
Service number 2/1
Battery sergeant major, D Battery,
New Zealand Field Artillery Volunteers

Donald Jessen (1895–1919)
Service number 2/2848
New Zealand Field Artillery

William John Alfred Vetori (1893–1962)
Service number 61850
Private, 31st Reinforcements

Armanella Rebecha Walls (1896–1984)
William Samuel Alfred Vetori (1918–1943)

James Bury (unknown–1918)
Service number 265485
Sergeant, Duke of Wellington's Regiment
(West Riding), British Army

Albert Lionel Bailey (1894–1965)
Service number 24/361
Corporal, New Zealand Rifle Brigade

Acknowledgements

Berry Boys is the culmination of work by a number of people, not only from Te Papa's History team, but also the wider community.

We would like to thank Dr Claudia Orange for supporting the original project to identify the Berry soldiers, which was initiated by Te Papa historian Kirstie Ross and carried out with the support of Kiera Gould, an intern from Leicester University (UK), and curator Lynette Townsend. Thank you to Philip Edgar and Adrian Kingston from Te Papa's Digital Collections and Access team for introducing the History team to the power of crowd sourcing, and also to Athol McCredie, Lissa Mitchell and Anita Schrafft for their knowledge, care and curation of the actual Berry negatives.

Following media interest from the *Dominion Post*, Radio New Zealand and Television New Zealand's *Sunday* programme, to whom we are also greatly indebted, a group of volunteers joined the project. We would like to thank Lynley Goldsmith, Chris McLennan and Allan Dodson for their tenacious assistance, uniform expert Barry O'Sullivan for his knowledge of uniforms, and Christopher Pugsley for his invaluable peer review of the book during production.

A special thanks to William Berry's granddaughter, Jill Helson, who contacted us from Queensland, Australia, after being shown TVNZ's *Sunday* documentary, and who helped flesh out her grandfather William Berry's life for us. Thanks also to Delia Grace, who originally discovered the collection of Berry & Co. negatives, and to the current residents of 147 Cuba Street, and Wellington City Council Archives, for their assistance regarding the history of Berry & Co. and the building.

Institutionally, we are indebted to Tamaki Paenga Hira Auckland War Memorial Museum for its Cenotaph database, which is an excellent introductory portal for basic information on First World War personnel who served overseas; and to Archives New Zealand for its commitment to digitising all of the war service files, which are an incredibly rich resource for the details of an individual's service, from enlistment through to death or discharge.

Much information in the service files is handwritten, and notations were often scrawled in minute script by harried clerks who used abbreviations that are now unfamiliar. The New Zealand Defence Force's website was a useful aid in deciphering the abbreviations. The New Zealand Mounted Rifles Association's guide to the forty-three Reinforcements of the New Zealand Expeditionary Force that sailed to Europe and the Middle East was also useful.

We are thankful to the National Library for its 'Papers Past' website, which has revolutionised historical research in New Zealand by providing access to digitised newspapers and periodicals. For the First World War period, many local newspapers and some national publications, such as *New Zealand Truth* and the *Maoriland Worker*, are now digitised. Some metropolitan newspapers, such as the *Auckland Star*, the *New Zealand Herald* and Wellington's *Evening Post*, are accessible up to 1945, and this has facilitated efforts to follow up post-war lives of veterans and their families.

We are thankful to the Commonwealth War Graves Commission for the locations of burial places of those who did not come home, and memorials to the missing. We also acknowledge the many New Zealand local and regional councils who publish cemetery databases containing the burial places of veterans who did return to New Zealand. The Wellington cemeteries database was particularly useful to our project as many of the people depicted were Wellington locals.

We warmly acknowledge the team at Production Shed.TV for telling the Berry Boys' stories in a uniquely creative way, sure to reach many New Zealanders and help bring other families' stories to light in the future.

We would like to acknowledge the generous support of Wellington City Council's WW100 commemorative programme, and also Mainprint / Ultimo Group, who printed this book.

Thank you also to everyone who helped realise the book under pressure: Claire Murdoch and Hannah Newport-Watson from Te Papa Press, designer Spencer Levine, editor Matt Turner, proofreader Susi Bailey and indexer Ginny Sullivan.

Most of all, thank you to all the soldiers' family members who contacted us and shared their stories with us. This book is dedicated to you.

Notes

1. Caroline Brothers, *War and Photography: A cultural history*, Routledge, New York, 1997.
2. Auckland City Libraries, for example, hold a collection of 4500 soldier portraits by Auckland photographer Herman Schmidt. 'Herman John Schmidt', Auckand Libriaries, www.aucklandlibraries.govt.nz/EN/heritage/sirgeorgegrey/photographs/hermanjohnschmidt/Pages/hermanjohnschmidt.aspx, accessed 15 March 2014.
3. William Main, *Wellington Through a Victorian Lens Revisited*, Steele Roberts, Wellington, 2011, p. 192.
4. *Evening Post*, 7 November 1906, p. 2.
5. It is possible that Edward Freeman, who had been director of the New Zealand Photographic Company before it was acquired by William Berry, stayed on with Berry & Co. as a photographer or silent partner. In 1924, the name of the company changed to Berry-Freeman Co., and remained so until 1927.
6. *Free Lance*, 30 March 1901, p. 17.
7. Berry & Co.'s show window was broken into in 1910 by a drunk. *Dominion*, 29 October 1910, p. 14.
8. Personal correspondence with Jill Helson, William Berry's great-granddaughter, 10 March 2014.
9. *Evening Post*, 24 May 1888, p. 3.
10. *Wairarapa Daily Times*, 3 January 1890, p. 4.
11. *Evening Post*, 5 December 1902, p. 5; ibid., 11 January 1907, p. 1; ibid., 13 August 1908, p. 1.
12. Ibid., 20 December 1902, p. 2.
13. Main, p. 192.
14. *Free Lance*, 8 August 1914, p. 6.
15. *Dominion*, 18 August 1914, p. 6.
16. Greg Kerr, *Private Wars: Personal records of the Anzacs in the Great War*, Oxford University Press, South Melbourne, 2000, p. 13.
17. Song written by Frank Fay, Ben Ryan and Dave Dreyer, 1918, published by Harry von Tilzer Music Publishing Co., 1918.
18. *Evening Post*, 22 January 1900, p. 2.
19. Ibid.
20. *Evening Post*, 23 May 1888; p. 3. Ian McGibbon (ed.), *The Oxford Companion to New Zealand Military History*, Oxford University Press, Auckland, 2000, p. 569.
21. Diary of Private Arthur Reginald Sims, 5 January 1917 to 6 January 1918. Kippenberger Research Centre, National Army Museum, Waiouru. Accession No. 1990.1619.
22. Quoted in Kate Hunter and Kirstie Ross, *Holding on to Home: New Zealand stories and objects of the First World War*, Te Papa Press, Wellington, 2014, p. 33.
23. Bert Stokes to his mother, 12 and 27 July 1916. MS-Papers-46, 53-02, Alexander Turnbull Library, Wellington.
24. John Crawford (ed.), *No Better Death: The Great War diaries and letters of William G Malone*, Reed Books, Auckland, 2005, p. 252.
25. Sandy Callister, *The Face of War: New Zealand's Great War photography*, Auckland University Press, Auckland, 2008, p. 11.
26. Raphael Samuel, *Theatres of Memory, Vol. 1: Past and present in contemporary culture* (1996), Verso, London, 2012, p. 352.
27. Callister, p. 14.
28. Glyn Harper, *Images of War, World War One: A photographic record of New Zealanders at war, 1914–1918*, HarperCollins, Auckland, 2008, p. 21.
29. 'Dominion of New Zealand – facts and stats', New Zealand History Online, http://www.nzhistory.net.nz/war/new-zealand-facts, accessed 30 March 2014.
30. 'First World War casualties by month', New Zealand History Online, http://www.nzhistory.net.nz/media/photo/first-world-war-casualties-month, accessed 30 March 2014.
31. 'New Zealand Wounded', *The Register*, 5 July 1915, p. 9.
32. James Belich, *Paradise Reforged: A history of the New Zealanders from the 1880s to the year 2000*, Allen Lane/Penguin, Auckland, 2001, p. 100.
33. *NZ Truth*, 18 November 1916, p. 6.
34. *Dominion*, 3 March, 1911, p. 4.
35. National Archives of Australia, series B2455, Heward C N 2132.
36. 'First World War casualties by month', accessed 14 April 2014.
37. *Free Lance*, 13 October 1916, p. 19.
38. National Archives of Australia, series B2455, Heward C N 2132.
39. Callister, p. 11.
40. Susan Sontag, *On Photography*, Penguin, London, 1977, p. 15.
41. *Evening Post*, 3 August 1918, p. 1.
42. This contrasts with the Herman Schmidt collection, which came complete with registers.
43. Samuel, p. 328.

Bibliography

Websites

'Archway', Archives New Zealand,
http://www.archway.archives.govt.nz

'Birth, Death and Marriage Historical Records',
Department of Internal Affairs,
https://www.bdmhistoricalrecords.dia.govt.nz/Home

'Cemeteries search', Wellington City Council,
http://wellington.govt.nz/services/community-and-culture/
cemeteries/cemeteries-search

'Cenotaph database', Auckland War Memorial Museum,
http://muse.aucklandmuseum.com/databases/Cenotaph/307.detail

'Common British military abbreviations', The Long, Long Trail:
The British Army in the Great War of 1914–18,
http://www.1914-1918.net/abbrev.htm

Commonwealth War Graves Commission, http://www.cwgc.org/

'Dominion of New Zealand – facts and stats', New Zealand
History Online,
http://www.nzhistory.net.nz/war/new-zealand-facts

'Embarkations of reinforcements from New Zealand 1914–18',
New Zealand Mounted Rifles Association,
http://www.nzmr.org/lists/reinforce.html

'First World War Army Service Records: Commonly Used
Abbreviations', New Zealand Defence Force,
http://www.nzdf.mil.nz/personnel-records/nzdf-archives/resources/
ww1-army-service-records.htm

'First World War casualties by month', New Zealand History Online,
http://www.nzhistory.net.nz/media/photo/first-world-war-
casualties-month

'Herman John Schmidt', Auckand Libriaries,
http://www.aucklandlibraries.govt.nz/EN/heritage/sirgeorgegrey/
photographs/hermanjohnschmidt/Pages/hermanjohnschmidt

New Zealand Army Nursing Service,
http://www.nzans.org/index.htm

'Papers Past', National Library of New Zealand,
http://paperspast.natlib.govt.nz/cgi-bin/paperspast

'Ribbons of British Commonwealth War and Campaign Medals
Awarded to New Zealanders', New Zealand Defence Force,
http://medals.nzdf.mil.nz/category/h/ribbons.html

Te Ara/Encyclopedia of New Zealand, http://www.teara.govt.nz

Books

Austin, Lieutenant Colonel William Semmens, *The Official History of the New Zealand Rifle Brigade*, L T Watkins Ltd, Wellington, 1924, available at http://nzetc.victoria.ac.nz/tm/scholarly/tei-WH1-NZRi-t1-front-d1-d1.html

Belich, James, *Paradise Reforged: A history of the New Zealanders from the 1880s to the year 2000*, Allen Lane/ Penguin, Auckland, 2001.

Brothers, Caroline, *War and Photography: A cultural history*, Routledge, New York, 1997.

Byrne, Lieutenant John Richard, *New Zealand Artillery in the Field, 1914–18*, Whitcombe and Tombs Ltd., Auckland, 1922, available at http://nzetc.victoria.ac.nz/tm/scholarly/tei-WH1NZAr.html

Callister, Sandy, *The Face of War: New Zealand's Great War photography*, Auckland University Press, Auckland, 2008.

Corbett, David A, *The Regimental Badges of New Zealand*, published by the author, Auckland, 1970.

Crawford, John (ed.), *No Better Death: The Great War diaries and letters of William G Malone*, Reed Books, Auckland, 2005.

Crawford, John, and Ian McGibbon, *New Zealand's Great War: New Zealand, the Allies, and the First World War*, Exisle Publishing, Auckland, 2007.

Drew, Lieutenant Henry Thomas Bertie, *The War Effort of New Zealand*, Whitcombe and Tombs Ltd, Wellington, 1923, available at http://nzetc.victoria.ac.nz/tm/scholarly/tei-WH1-Effo-t1-front-d2-d1.html

Harper, Glyn, *Images of War, World War One: A photographic record of New Zealanders at war, 1914–1918*, HarperCollins, Auckland, 2008.

Henderson, Alan, David Green and Peter DF Cooke, *The Gunners: A History of New Zealand artillery*, Raupo Books (an imprint of Penguin Books NZ), Auckland, 2008.

Hunter, Kate, and Kirstie Ross, *Holding on to Home: New Zealand stories and objects of the First World War*, Te Papa Press, Wellington, 2014.

Hutchinson, Garrie, *Pilgrimage: A traveller's guide to New Zealanders in two world wars*, Penguin, Auckland, 2012.

Kerr, Greg, *Private Wars: Personal records of the Anzacs in the Great War*, Oxford University Press, South Melbourne, 2000.

Luxford, Major John Hector, *With the Machine Gunners in France and Palestine*, Whitcombe and Tombs Ltd, Auckland, 1923, http://nzetc.victoria.ac.nz/tm/scholarly/tei-WH1-Mach-t1-front-d4-d1.html

McGibbon, Ian (ed.), *The Oxford Companion to New Zealand Military History*, Oxford University Press, Auckland, 2000.

McLean, Gavin, *The White Ships: New Zealand's First World War hospital ships*, New Zealand Ship & Marine Society, Wellington, 2013.

Main, William, *Wellington Through a Victorian Lens Revisited*, Steele Roberts, Wellington, 2011.

O'Sullivan, Barry, and Matthew O'Sullivan, *New Zealand Army Personal Equipment 1910–1945*, Wilson Scott Publishing, Christchurch, 2005.

O'Sullivan, Barry, and Matthew O'Sullivan, *New Zealand Army Uniforms and Clothing 1910–1945*, Wilson Scott Publishing, Christchurch, 2009.

Rice, Geoffrey, with assistance from Linda Bryder, *Black November: The 1918 influenza pandemic in New Zealand*, second edition, Canterbury University Press, Christchurch, 2005.

Samuel, Raphael, *Theatres of Memory, Vol. 1: Past and present in contemporary culture* (1996), Verso, London, 2012.

Sontag, Susan, *On Photography*, Penguin, London, 1977.

Stewart, Colonel Hugh, *The New Zealand Division, 1916–1919*, Whitcombe and Tombs Ltd., Auckland, 1921, available at http://nzetc.victoria.ac.nz/tm/scholarly/tei-WH1-Fran.html

Thomas, Malcolm, and Cliff Lord, *New Zealand Army Distinguishing Patches 1911–1991* (two parts), published by the authors, Wellington, 1995.

Treanor, Kenneth Robert, *The Staff, the Serpent and the Sword: 100 years of the Royal New Zealand Army Medical Corps*, Wilson Scott Publishing, Christchurch, 2008.

Unpublished sources

Bert Stokes to his mother, 12 and 27 July 1916. MS-Papers-46, 53-02, Alexander Turnbull Library, Wellington.

Diary of Private Arthur Reginald Sims, 5 January 1917 to 6 January 1918. Kippenberger Research Centre, National Army Museum, Waiouru. Accession No. 1990.1619.

National Archives of Australia, series B2455, Heward C N 2132.

Index

Entries in **bold** refer to illustrations

5th (Wellington Rifles) Regiment **15**, 26, 32, 68
64 Cuba Street, Wellington 2
147 Cuba Street, Wellington 1, **1**, 4, 15

Anderson, Marion 154, **155**
Anderson, William 154, **155**
Anzac Day
    parades 118
    wreaths 22
Anzac soldier, myth of 12
'Armes' (unidentified solider) **25**
Armistice Day celebrations
    Levin 14
    Masterton 14
Ashburton 140
Auckland 1, 9, 25, 32, 74, 86, 108, 116, 134, 142, 150
    see also Crown Studios
Auckland Hospital 52
Auckland Infantry Regiment 74, 86, 88, 114, 172
Auckland–Wellington Regiment 70, 78, 88
Australian Imperial Force 12

backgrounds, photographic 4, **5**
Baigent, Annie 66, **67**
Baigent, Ashley Heath 66, **67**
Bailey, Albert 182, **183**
Baker, Cecil Charles 34, **35**
Baker, Hannah Irene 34, **35**
Ballinger, Claude Carey **96**, 97
Ballinger, Ivy Hilda **96**
balloting 12, 92, 120, 166
Bank of New South Wales' Roll of Honour **10**
'Banks' (unidentified family) 130, **131**
Bapaume, Second Battle of 106
Barber, Francis 146, **147**
Bates, William Henry 46, **47**
Batten, Harold John 90, **91**
Battersby, Gladys Francis Maude 166, **167**
Battersby, Richard Weir 166, **167**
Beaufort, Francis Edward **70**, 72, **73**
Beckett, Helen Mary 36, **37**
Beckett, Middleton **10**, 36, **36**, **37**

Berrold, Charles *see* Vandersluys, Charles Caleb
Berry and Co., Wellington 1, **1**, 4, 8–9, 10, 15, 18, 36, 60, 65, 76, 88, 114, 124, 131, 134, 138, 140, 148, 178, 183
Berry, Beatrice **2**, 12, 14
Berry, Elizabeth 'Lizzie' **2**, 4, 14
Berry, Ethel **2**, 12
Berry, Florence **2**, 12, 14–15
Berry, Mabel **2**, 12, 14
Berry, William 1, 2, **2**, 4, 8, 12, 14, 15
Berry, William Keith 50, **51**
Beu, Frederick Lars John 172, **173**
Bevan, William Charles 38, **39**
Blyth, Alick 158, **159**
Blyth, Maud Allison 158, **159**
'Bolton' (unidentified couple) **65**
Bowker, William James Leonard 134, **135**
Boyd, James Hall 174, **175**
Boyd, James Robert 174, **175**
Boyd, Mary Louisa 174, **175**
Braddock, Jack Langley 76, **77**
'Briggs' (unidentified solider) 24, **25**
British Army 26, 54, 178, 183
British War Medal 56, 74
Briton (troopship) 128
'Brooks' (unidentified solider) **25**
'Brown' (unidentified family) 130, **131**
Burch, George Robert 164, **165**
Bury, James 182, **183**

C1 training camp and draft 152, 156, 172
cabinet photographs **2**, 9, 65, 158
'Callum' (unidentified couple) **65**
cameras, soldiers' 7
Cannock Chase War Cemetery, England 154
Canterbury Infantry Battalion 34, 48
Canterbury Infantry Regiment 40, 86, 98, 102, 140
Carterton, Wairarapa 72
casualties 14
    on Gallipoli 10, 98
    on Western Front 36, 40, 48, 78, 90, 114
casualty lists 9, 10, **10**
cemeteries, military *see* Cannock Chase War Cemetery, England; Heliopolis War Cemetery, Egypt; Lijssenthoek Military Cemetery, Belgium; Motor Car Corner Military Cemetery, Belgium

Chesnutt, Creighton 124, **125**
'Chiss', or 'Hiss', or 'McNiss' (unidentified family) **131**
Chote, Arthur 102, **103**
Chunuk Bair, Gallipoli 26, 30, 146
Clay, John Owen 40, **41**
Coate, Cecil Theobald 78, **79**
conscription 12, 78
    opposition to 140
copies, of photographs 183
Cornes, Arthur Dudley 74, **75**
Cornes, Dorothy Bertha 74, **74**, **75**
Costello, Frederick 48, **49**
Costello, Herbert 48, **49**
Costello, William 48, **49**
costumes, in use in photographs **5**, 7
'Cotter' (unidentified solider) **25**
Cresswell, Sidney 54, **55**
Crichton, William 2
cropping, of photographs 7
Crossan, John Blair 82, **83**
Crown Studios, Auckland 9
Cuba Photographers, Wellington 1

Dannevirke 102
Defence Department 56, 58, 74, 118, 138, 168
Denniston, George **9**
diaries, soldiers' 9
Distinguished Conduct Medal 26
Divisional Signallers 148
dry plate negatives 4, 64
Dunedin 1, 98, 108, 170, 180
Duntroon, South Canterbury 58

exposures, multiple 26

fathers, of soldiers 12
Faulkner, Charles Henry 98, **99**
Faulkner, Edith 98, **99**
Faulkner, Edwin 98, **99**
Faulkner, Eslet 98, **99**
Featherston, Wairarapa 30, 128
    see also Pihautea Returned Soldiers' Settlement
Featherston prisoner-of-war camp 26
Feilding 92
Field Punishment No. 2 50

Fiji 134
Freeman, Herbert James 128, **129**
Freeman, Marguerita 128, **129**
Freeman, Zena 128, **129**
fund-raising 7, **13**, 14
    see also Soldiers' Christmas Gift Fund
Gallipoli **9**, 10, 18, 20, 22, 25, 26, 28, 30, 32, 34, 98, 118, 120, 136, 146, 162
    see also Chunuk Bair
Gamon, Amy 162, **163**
Gamon, Arthur 162, **163**
Gamon, Kathleen 162, **163**
Gempton, William **11**
Gillham, James 100, **101**
Girl Peace Scouts 7
Gisborne 22, 52, 170
    see also Waerenga-o-Kuri
Gisborne Herald (newspaper) 26
glass plate negatives 4, **8**, 9, 15
Goetzlof, R 1
Goldfinch, Adolph 80, **81**
Goldfinch, Ann 80, **81**
Goldfinch, Arthur **81**
Goldfinch, Charles **81**
Goldfinch, Eileen **81**
Goldfinch, James **81**
Gollins, Grace Caroline 140, **141**
Gollins, Graham 140, **141**
Gollins, Thomas Christopher 140, **141**
Gordonton, Waikato 88
Gower, Alfred Featherston 104, **105**, 106
Gower, Gerald 104, **104**, 106, **107**
Grace, Delia 1
Graham, Eric Richard Davies 168, **169**
'Graham' (unidentified family) **131**
'Green' (unidentified couple) 64, **65**

hairdressers, at photographic studios 4, **4**
Hamilton 80, 90, 106, 128
Hamilton, Muriel May 170, **171**
Hamilton, Thomas Shaw 170, **171**
Hardham, William James 118
'Harris' (unidentified girl) **7**, 44
'Harris' (unidentified solider) 44, **45**
Harrison, Henri 1, 15
Hart, Alfred 142, **143**
Hart, Queenie 142, **143**
Hawera, Taranaki 26, 68, 140
Hawker, Leslie John 150, **151**
Hawke's Bay 84

Hawke's Bay Regiment 26
Helensville, Kaipara Harbour 1, 86
Heliopolis War Cemetery, Egypt 176
'Henderson' (unidentified family) 130, **131**
'Henderson' (unidentified solider) 44, **45**, 130, **131**
Heward, Claude **12**, 14–15
Hoffer, Elliott 94, **95**
Home Guard 42, 88
Hornig brothers 12
Hornig, George Gordon Campbell 18, **19**
Hornig, William Francis 18, **18**
horses and mules, use of in war 38, 58, 116, 142
Houchen, Roy 20, **21**
Hoverd, Florence Lilian 152, **153**
Hoverd, James Arthur 152, **153**
'Howe' (unidentified couple) 64, **65**

Independent Order of Odd Fellows 20
influenza 50, 54, 68, 126, 136, 140, 154
insignia and badges, military 15, **15**, 36, 48, 62, 65, 68, 88, 92, 108, 114, 124, 131, 144, 150, 166, 168
Ionic (troopship) 116, 166

James, Gertrude Miriam 26, **27**
James, William Horace 26, **27**
Jessen, Donald 182, **183**
Jessen, John 182, **183**
Jewish soldiers 94
Juno, James Arthur 30, **31**

Karori Cemetery, Wellington 126
Kaywood, John William 32, **33**
King George V Hospital, Rotorua 116
King's South Africa War Medal 170

Larkin, William Alexander 136, **137**
Legion of Frontiersmen 18, 22
'lemon-squeezer' hats 64, 76, **77**, 150, **151**, **182**
letters home 8, 10
Levin 140
    see also Armistice Day celebrations
Lijssenthoek Military Cemetery, Belgium 76

Liverpool, Lady 7
Luckman, Ellen Isabella 92, **93**
Luckman, Harry 92, **93**
Luckman, Harry George 92, **93**

McLeavey, Peter 1
Maheno (New Zealand Hospital Ship No. 1) 46
Main, William John 86, **87**
Makara Cemetery, Wellington 92
Malone, William 9, 10
Malta (troopship) 68
Managh, Margaret Young 114, **115**
Managh, Robert 114, **115**
Mangateparu, Morrinsville 42
Marama (New Zealand Hospital Ship No. 2) 46, 142, 160
Mararoa (Wellington–Lyttelton steamer) 176
Marchant, Eric Edward 132, **133**
Martinborough, Wairarapa 116
Marton, Rangitikei District 98, 114
Mason, Kenneth Randall 148, **149**
Masterton, Wairarapa 65, 128, 142, 164
    see also Armistice Day celebrations
Matatua (troopship) 166
Matheson, Ethel Louisa Gertrude 108, **109**
Matheson, James Alexander 108, **109**
Maunganui (troopship) 48, 58, 90, 120
Mauriceville, Wairarapa 183
medals *see* British War Medal; Distinguished Conduct Medal; King's South Africa War Medal; Meritorious Service Medal; Military Medal; Queen Victoria Jubilee Medal; Queen's South Africa War Medal; South Africa 1902 clasp; Victoria Cross; Victory Medal
medical examinations 12
Mediterranean–Aegean theatre of war 46
Melton, William Edward 176, **177**
memorials and memorial cards **10**, 22, 76, 120, 154, 183
    see also Bank of New South Wales' Roll of Honour; mourning process, and photographs
Meritorious Service Medal 50
Messines, battle at 26, 42, 114, 154
Military Medal 72, 146
Mitchell, Edwin 138, **139**

Mokoia (troopship) 110
Morgan, Edmund Guthrie 28, **28**, **29**
Morgan, Francis Harold 28, **28**, **29**
Morgan, Joyce Veda 28, **29**
Mossman, Esther Muriel 22, **23**
Mossman, Marion Susan 22, **23**
Mossman, Thomas Henry 22, **23**
Motor Car Corner Military Cemetery, Belgium 70
mourning process, and photographs 1, 10, 14
'Murray' (unidentified solider) 44, **45**

Napier 36, 48, 50, 174, 183
Nelson 62, 66, 84, 150, 152, 176
New Zealand Army Medical Corps **15**, 20, 46, 50, 64, 146, 160, 162, 174
New Zealand Army Ordnance Corps 134, 136, 138, 180
New Zealand Army Service Corps 58, 74
New Zealand Dental Corps 108
New Zealand Expeditionary Force (NZEF) **15**, 18, 20, 34, 48, 54, 150, 158, 172
New Zealand Field Artillery 32, 38, 66, 82, 110, 118, 120, 122, 142, 168, 183
New Zealand Field Artillery Volunteers 183
New Zealand Garrison Artillery 118, 120, 132
New Zealand Garrison Artillery Volunteers 20, 168
New Zealand Infantry Brigade 150
New Zealand Machine Gun Corps 114, 140, 176
New Zealand Military Police 178
New Zealand Mounted Rifles Brigade 40, 68
New Zealand Photographic Company 2, 4, 8
New Zealand Pioneer Battalion 54
New Zealand Police Force 124
New Zealand Rifle Brigade 36, 42, 48, 50, 60, 76, 84, 90, 94, 104, 106, 128, 144, 164, 183
New Zealand Veterinary Corps 38, 68
No. 1 New Zealand Field Ambulance 112
No. 1 New Zealand General Hospital, Brockenhurst 38, 56, 62, 86, 112
No. 2 New Zealand General Hospital, Walton-on-Thames 50, 72, 84, 90, 98, 104

No. 3 New Zealand General Hospital, Codford 82, 84, 96, 106, 112, 114
No. 30 Company (Wellington Technical School) Senior Cadets 18
Normanby, Taranaki 82
Norsewood, Tararua District 36
NZEF *see* New Zealand Expeditionary Force

O'Brien, Kathleen **13**
'Oliver' (unidentified solider) 24, **25**
Otago Infantry Battalion 162
Otago Infantry Regiment 100, 124
Otaki, Kapiti Coast 90

Pahiatua, Tararua District 72
Pakeha (troopship) 82, 90
Palestine 68, 176
Palmerston North 94
'Parks' (unidentified solider) **45**
Parliamentary Recruiting Committee **6**
Passchendaele (Third Battle of Ypres) 26, 48, 62, 72, 76, 78, 90, 92
patriotic revues **13**
Petone 60, 106, 126
photographic studios and photographers 1, 2, **3**, 4
   see also Berry and Co.; Crown Studios; Cuba Photographers; Goetzlof, R; Harrison, Henri; New Zealand Photographic Company; Zak's photographic studio
photographs, of civilians who had been soldiers 148, **148**
photographs, of couples 1, 12, 64, **65**, 66, **67**, 74, **75**, 86, **87**, 108, **109**, 112, **113**, 114, **115**, 122, **123**, 158, **159**, 160, **161**, 166, **167**, 170, **171**
   see also photography, wedding
photographs, of families 1, **2**, 9, 10, 12, 14, 22, **23**, 28, **29**, 36, **37**, 48, **49**, 80, **81**, 92, **93**, 98, **99**, 120, **121**, 128, **129**, **130**, 131, 140, **141**, 154, **155**, 162, **163**, 174, **175**
photographs, of soldiers 1, 7, 9–10, **11**, 12, 14, *passim*
photographs, of soldiers' sweethearts 10
photographs, taken by soldiers 8, **9**, 10
photography, wedding 4, 12, 34, **35**, 42, **43**, 68, **69**, 96, 142, **143**, 152, **153**

Pihautea Returned Soldiers' Settlement, Featherston 30
Pilkington, Harold 112, **113**
plein-air photographs **182**, 183
'Porter' (unidentified solider) 24, **25**
portraiture 2, 4, **4**, **5**, 8, 9, 10, 26
postcards 9, 158
Powell, Harry Spire 110, **111**
props, photographic 4, **5**
Prussing, William John Adam 84, **85**

Queen Victoria Jubilee Medal 138
Queen's South Africa War Medal 170

Reeve, Ernest Walter 116, **117**
Reinforcements
   2nd 22, 42
   4th 26, 28, 131
   6th 34
   7th 38
   8th 25
   11th 40
   12th 52, 54
   14th 58
   16th 60, 116
   17th 108
   21st 62
   23rd 68, 70, 72, 74
   24th 68, 78, 80, 82, 84, 90, 98
   25th 66, 78, 86, 88, 92, 94
   26th 94, 96
   27th 102, 124
   28th 100, 102, 104, 106, 122, 124, 140
   29th 110, 114
   30th 25, 112, 114
   31st 166, 183
   32nd 28, 116, 118, 120, 122
   33rd 65, 124
   34th 112, 158
   37th 166
   38th 142
   39th 148
   40th 150, 160, 172
   41st 154, 164, 176
   42nd 128, 152, 154, 164
   43rd 152, 166
   44th 172
   45th 162, 168, 172
   47th 156

Reinforcements *continued*
    48th 170
    49th 168
    50th 172
retouching 4
Returned Services' Association (RSA) 42, 118
Roberts, Pryce 56, **57**
Roberts, William George 60, **61**
Robinson, Edmund Colin Nigel 42, **43**
Robinson, Mary Theresa Veronica 42, **43**
Royal Engineers forestry companies 54
Royal Marine Light Infantry 138
Royal New Zealand Air Force 140
Royal New Zealand Artillery 25, 134, 168
    see also New Zealand Field Artillery; New Zealand Field Artillery Volunteers; New Zealand Garrison Artillery; New Zealand Garrison Artillery Volunteers
Royal New Zealand Engineers 18, 28, 56, 60

Samoa, defence of 28, 132
Scambary, Arthur James 120, 122, **123**
Scambary, George Eric **8**, 120, **121**
Scambary, Ida Emily **8**, 120, **121**
Scambary, Mary 122, **123**
Scambary, Walter George **8**, 120, **121**, 122
Scott, George Mackay 144, **145**
Second World War 15, 26, 28, 42, 50, 60, 72, 88, 92, 134, 140, 150, 176
shell shock 92, 142
signallers 86, 148
'Simpson' (unidentified family) 12, **131**
Sims, Arthur 9
Smith, Frederick David Mason 118, **119**
Soldiers' Christmas Gift Fund 14
Somme, Battle of the 14, 40, 50, 142, 154, 183
songs, First World War 7–8
South Africa 1902 clasp 170
South African (Second Boer) War 18, 52, 118, 170, 178
Stewart, Thomas Fleming 70, **71**
Stokes, Bert 9, 10
Stratford, Taranaki **3**, 68, 106
stretcher-bearers 146
suicide 120, 142
Sutherland, Gordon Grant 58, **59**
Tahiti (troopship) 92, 94, 116, 120

Taihape, Rangitikei 124
Takaka, Golden Bay 66
    see also Waitapu, Takaka
Taranaki 42, 56, 70, 104, 124, 140, 146, 174
    see also Hawera; Stratford
Taylor, John Frederick 68, **69**
Taylor, Maud Florence 68, **69**
Te Awamutu, Waikato 106
Te Kuiti, Waikato 48
Territorial Training Scheme 18, 116
Tofua (troopship) 128, 164
Turnbull, Charles McLaren 160, **161**
Turnbull, Evelyn Hilda 160, **161**

Ulimaroa (troopship) 62, 80
unidentified couples 64, **65**
unidentified families 130, **131**
unidentified soldiers 24, **25**, 44, **45**, 70, **71**
uniforms, soldiers' 15, 22, 25, 108

Vandersluys, Charles Caleb **178**, **179**
Vaughan, John Edgar 62, **63**
venereal disease (VD) 20, 82, 106
Vetori, Armanella Rebecha **182**, **183**
Vetori, William John Alfred **182**, **183**
Vetori, William Samuel Alfred **182**, **183**
Victoria Cross 118
Victory Medal 56, 74
Vincent, Percy Alfred 52, **53**
voluntary enlistment 6

Wadestown, Wellington 166
Waerenga-o-Kuri, Gisborne 22
Wager, Louis 126, **127**
Waikanae, Kapiti Coast 110
Waikato *see* Gordonton; Te Awamutu; Te Kuiti
Waikato Regiment 24
Wairarapa *see* Carterton; Featherston; Martinborough; Masterton; Mauriceville
Waitapu, Takaka 62
Walker, John McVean 180, **181**
Wanden, William John 156, **157**
'Watt' (unidentified couple) 64, **65**
Wellington 1–2, 4, 7, 8, 9, 10, 12, 14, 18, 20, 22, 25, 28, 32, 34, 36, 38, 40, 46, 48, 54, 56, 60, 65, 76, 78, 80, 86, 94, 96, 98, 100, 102, 110, 116, 118, 120, 122, 124, 126, 131, 132, 136, 138, 140, 142, 144, 146, 148, 150, 152, 154, 156, 160, 162, 164, 168, 174, 180, 183
    see also 64 Cuba Street; 147 Cuba Street; Cuba Photographers; Karori Cemetery; Makara Cemetery; Wadestown; Zak's photographic studio
Wellington Infantry Battalion 26, 28, 30
Wellington Infantry Regiment 26, 30, 52, 70, 72, 78, 80, 112
Wellington Mounted Rifles 104
Western Front 25, 32, 36, 46, 52, 56, 76, 84, 88, 102, 104, 120, 142, 146, 162, 176
    see also Bapaume, Second Battle of; Messines, battle at; Passchendaele (Third Battle of Ypres); Somme, Battle of the
Westport 34, 154
Whanganui 114, 130
'Wilcox' (unidentified solider) 44, **45**
Williamson, Richard Arthur 88, **89**
Willochra (troopship) 10, 94

YMCA **12**, 14
Ypres, Belgium 25, 62, 76
    see also Lijssenthoek Military Cemetery; Passchendaele (Third Battle of Ypres)

Zak's photographic studio, Wellington 183